Signs of Agni Yoga
BROTHERHOOD

BROTHERHOOD

1937

Agni Yoga Society
319 West 107th Street
New York NY 10025
www.agniyoga.org

© 1962 by the Agni Yoga Society.
Published 1962.

Reprinted 2017. Updated August 2021.
Translated from Russian by the Agni Yoga Society.

ISBN: 978-1-946742-88-9
ISBN (eBook): 978-1-946742-24-7

That which is most sacred surrounds the concept of Brotherhood.

That which is most joyful lives in the consciousness that there exists cooperation of Knowledge.

Such thought affirms that somewhere there are living True Co-workers.

Let us recall the fundamentals which lead to Brotherhood.

BROTHERHOOD

1. Let us consider a concept which has become extremely overburdened. Amidst daily life people assimilate with difficulty an understanding of cooperation, yet much more difficult and inaccessible to them is the concept of Brotherhood. Bodily heritage, that is, blood relationship, impedes the acceptance of the concept of Brotherhood. It is simpler for people to disclaim altogether any understanding of World Brotherhood. They would rather call it a utopia than reflect about the possibility of applying it in life.

If even in the narrow domain of domestic life people do not find within themselves the affirmation of brotherhood, then in the wider sense it may seem to them to be impractical. Besides, people read carelessly the ancient Scriptures, which speak about great numbers of Brothers and Sisters.

Likewise, people's recollections of the Subtle World have become clouded. Only there is it possible to encounter the expanded realization of Brotherhood. The body impedes the way to many broad ideas. Only by going beyond the limits of the bodily understanding is it possible to recognize brotherly cooperation. Let us gather the signs of such an expanded state of consciousness.

2. People have attempted to seal the union of brotherhood with blood. They have given up their most precious substance for the purpose of attaining the status of Brotherhood. Harkening to all the songs about Brotherhood one perceives a wondrous poem of the dreams of humanity. If one assembles all the cus-

toms which have been accumulated around the concept of Brotherhood one arrives at an extraordinarily touching testimony about the aspirations of peoples. The manifestation of achievements in the name of Brotherhood reveals that self-renunciation has been always linked with these endeavors of the pure heart. Yet precisely the concept of Brotherhood is especially desecrated and debased.

3. Even the best additions to the concept of Brotherhood have only lowered it and made it difficult to attain. It has been linked with liberty and equality, but this trinity was conceived in the earthly meaning, that is to say, under conditions in which neither freedom nor equality do exist.

The loftiest freedom can be realized in the Supermundane World, where laws are understood as a beautiful and immutable reality. There, too, equality of the seed of the spirit is understood, it being the sole measure of liberality and balance. Usually the earthly statues depicting liberty are furnished with wings or torches, thus reminding us about the higher spheres and conditions.

About images representing equality there is this anecdote: When a sculptor once received an order to execute a thousand statues depicting equality, to be used to decorate a triumphal avenue, he made one statue and proposed casting all the others from it.

4. Rarely is it possible to converse about Brotherhood. Precisely in the periods of great earthly obduracy it is not unusual to observe that people, as it were, have agreed to debase this very concept. Already the ancient customs of brotherhood through blood union have been turned into such menaces to the entire human race that the most primitive revenge may be regarded as a childish prank.

You know that I am speaking about something that is in particular need of reinforcement.

5. If you enter a gathering of people with the words, "Friends and co-workers," the majority will look upon you with suspicion. But if you dare to call them brothers and sisters, then most likely you will be denounced as having uttered inadmissible terms.

People sometimes establish brotherhoods, but such superficial and pompous institutions have nothing in common with the great concept of Brotherhood. Thus people start communities, cooperatives, various unions and societies; but in their foundations there will not be even simple trust. Consequently, these establishments are very remote from that Brotherhood which would be a strong and steadfast union of trust.

It may be that right now certain finer hearts are already dreaming about the creation of organizations where trust would be the cornerstone. It cannot be insisted that everything is bad, when the human eye sees only some of the details of the approaching epoch.

Upon the fragments of ancient symbols one may observe the vitality of the basic concepts. Just when from the earthly point of view everything has been transgressed, it may be that at the same time most beautiful concepts are already being born.

6. When, then, should one speak about the necessary concepts? Particularly when they have been transgressed. Precisely, then, let us speak about them when people already consider them hopeless. Why do We remind about Brotherhood just at present? Because people in their despair will come to seek the scattered seeds of the predestined Brotherly Community. Let us not be confused by the oscillations of the pendulum of life. Despair may be the forerunner of recovery of vision.

7. Rightly has it been observed that certain rays are apprehended with especial difficulty, as is also everything connected with these rays. That is why We do not try to coerce an alien consciousness that has been attuned differently. Compulsion is not an attribute of conviction. It is impossible to command friendship, and especially does this apply to brotherhood. These concepts require selflessness and an understanding of fundamentals.

If the broad concept of Brotherhood has come down to blood relationship, this means that the consciousness has become greatly impoverished. Often the consciousness is so limited that people cannot understand at all what manner of brotherhood could exist outside of blood kinship. Degrees of kinship have been designated, such as "first cousin," "second cousin," and even "third cousin," but further the imagination hesitates to proceed. Many books could be compiled of conventionalities that have piled up around the concept of Brotherhood.

In ages past many different peoples have emphasized the significance of Brotherhood. Fratricide was considered a grave crime. Behind all this could be discerned a reverence for a certain exalted status; with strong measures the people safeguarded something which had no place in their everyday thoughts. Reason denied this "something," but the heart in the depths of its fire affirmed it. The heart palpitated with the beauty of the meaning of Brotherhood. Again humanity will turn to the heart and will apprehend the essence of Brotherhood.

Perhaps Brotherhood does exist? Perhaps, as an earthly anchor, it maintains equilibrium? Perhaps in the dreams of humanity it has remained as an unalterable reality? Let us recall certain dreams and visions, so clearly engraved upon the memory, visions of walls and towers of the Brotherhood. The imagination is but a memory of that which exists.

Perhaps someone will remember also in reality the Tower of Chun?

8. The spark of Infinity must be expressed in everything. Each concept must include presupposition of its development into Infinity. There may be noted whole series of concepts which succeed each other. Neither friendship nor cooperation can be terminal. Between them and the Subtle World there must be still another something that can equally belong to the two worlds. This something is called Brotherhood.

No greater concept can be named, none which could so crown human relations and correspond to the essential nature of the Subtle and Fiery Worlds. Therefore the Brotherhood is called threefold. It extends between the three worlds as a firm bridge. It is almost impossible to imagine the contact of the earthly with the Fiery World, but under the panoply of Brotherhood such confluence is made possible.

9. No one wishes to find himself in an enclosed field with no possibility of even looking over the fence. One needs to discover a crack, though it be but a small one, through which to perceive the possibility of approach to Infinity. Even in daily life let there be found the unifying principle, so that not only the very small but also the great can be generally accepted.

Perhaps on each planet there is a place for great encounters.

10. When rocks begin to crumble people break them up and remove them for the security of the road; and so it is with certain human definitions. In the course of centuries a term may lose its original meaning and should be replaced by a word closer to the current period. This has happened with the word initiated. Together with anointment, its original meaning has been relegated to the past. Instead of initiated and uninitiated, let us say knowing and unknowing, or cognizant and ignorant. But it is better to express initiation itself by the word education. Thus it can be expressed without belittlement, in a word closer to contemporary times.

In no way is it right to conceal something good in outmoded words when it is possible to express it more comprehensibly for broad masses of people. Surely, knowledge is not for the elect but for all! Therefore, we should not reiterate outworn morals, but rather, designate the best conditions for scientific cognizance. Only the ignorant will not understand that for the successful advancement of science the best conditions of life must be established.

Science cannot go beyond the limits of the mechanistic circle so long as this wall remains unsurmounted by the understanding of the Subtle World.

11. In some places homeopathic remedies are forbidden; likewise, some insist upon curing people by their own methods only. Prohibitive thinking is limited. It is impossible to establish forbiddance of all but a single method of treatment. It should be remembered that all medicines are merely auxiliary expedients; without the primary energy no medicine will have the necessary effect.

It is impossible to divide physicians into allopaths and homeopaths, as each of them individually applies his best method. But the physician should be acquainted with the basic energy, which will be the operative factor for the speediest recovery.

12. It will be asked, "What connection is there between curative treatment, or outworn concepts, and our discourses about Brotherhood?" But light should be thrown upon the relationships of many concepts, which will broaden the understanding of Brotherhood.

13. On the paths to the Brotherhood let us fortify ourselves with trust. We are not speaking about some sort of blind faith but precisely about the quality of trust. It must be understood that our qualities are the habitat for vitamins. The quality of mistrust or doubt will be deadly for the best vitamins. Why saturate ourselves with manufactured vitamins, when we ourselves prove to be the best producers of them, and of the most powerful ones?

When external vitamins find themselves in a natural habitat, they can produce the full measure of reaction. But even the best vegetable vitamins cannot manifest their best properties when they enter a poisoned organism. Thus, We esteem those organisms in which the basic qualities of human nature have found application.

The being who is filled with doubt is not fit for even a primitive form of cooperation. He cannot even understand all the beautiful discipline of Brotherhood. Precisely discipline, as not otherwise can be named that voluntary harmony which lies in the foundation of the Brotherhood's labors. The Brothers join together for work, and without trust there would be no quality in their labor.

14. The Subtle World is frequently described as something misty, cold, a realm of wandering shadows. Do not such descriptions issue from superstition? Yet may they not result from inability to enjoy the advantages of the qualities of this superior state? Actually prejudice and mistrust can conceal the true aspect of the Subtle World. Even in the earthly condition man sees what he wishes to; then the more does he

see thus in that world where everything is composed of thought. There the dwellers can create and behold according to the quality of their thinking.

It is useful to possess pure thinking, as it knows indeed the meaning of trust.

15. A powerful energy has been released from a single spark. Likewise, from a flash of nerve force there can be established a constant influx of forces. People long ago realized that an onset of nerve energy is far more powerful than muscular force. It was avowed that the nerve tension is brief and is followed by a breakdown of forces. But such a postulate is not natural. Only the conditions of earthly life prevent a continuous replenishing with psychic energy. It is possible to create such conditions of life that psychic energy will be proportional with muscular energy. After the principle is discovered its expansion will be sought. Likewise, cooperation will not be limited to temporary flashes but will enter the consciousness, followed by Brotherhood. It is unwise to entrust a precious vessel to an inexperienced messenger. Likewise it is impossible for the Brotherhood to summon incognizant people. It is impossible for a balloon to sustain unlimited pressures without testing. Without steadfast realization people cannot take upon themselves the burden of the larger concepts. Even a horse is gradually accustomed to carrying loads. But if the spark of realization already shines, then the bearing of the rest of the load becomes progressively possible.

16. Some people talk little about Brotherhood but do much for it. And there are others who always have Brotherhood on their tongues and are never far from treachery.

17. Brotherhood must be looked upon as an institution wherein the members work not by day but by the task. One must love the labor in order to prefer the task work. It must be realized that the tasks are infinite and the process of perfectment is also unending. Whoever is afraid cannot grow to love labor.

You have sometimes listened to the beautiful singing of workers. Verily, work can be accompanied by both joy and inspired thought. But one must test oneself for everything.

18. On the paths to Brotherhood self-renunciation also will be needed. It is most likely that many will find such a condition difficult to fulfill. They do not realize how often people manifest this quality even in everyday life. In each inspiration, in each burst of enthusiasm, self-renunciation infallibly will be included. One should very precisely perceive the significance of words.

There do not exist in life any such qualities as would appertain exclusively to heroes. The fact is that heroes are not rare, but they are not always armed with swords and spears. Thus, it is necessary to understand and bring into life the best concepts.

One can deprive oneself of courage and steadfastness when one begins to repeat to oneself about difficulties of fulfillment. It makes no difference how courage is applied, it must grow untiringly. Instead of speaking about broken courage, it would be better for people to call this condition simply faint-heartedness. Bones and muscles can be broken, but the spirit is unbreakable! The faint-hearted and wavering man cannot serve the Brotherhood.

Self-renunciation is nothing else but inspiration; faint-heartedness cannot be inspiration.

19. Let us not take obstinacy along with us. There is no more intolerable burden than stubbornness. People do not even choose a headstrong horse; they will not even take an obstinate dog on a journey. Stubbornness is a paralysis of the best centers. Experiments with psychic energy will be without results if the investigator be stubborn.

Reason and wisdom contain no restrictive stubbornness.

20. Touchiness is not suitable for a long journey. This does not mean that We seek only supernal perfections. We merely forewarn as to what load should not be taken along. One should succeed in being fortified with joy, and in testing it in diverse circumstances and in all kinds of weather. One should not torture and torment oneself, but one should make tests in order to ascertain the measure of one's bodily endurance.

21. Any food containing blood is harmful for the development of subtle energy. If humanity would only refrain from devouring dead bodies, then evolution could be accelerated. Meat lovers have tried to remove the blood, but they have not been able to obtain the desired results. Meat, even with the blood removed, cannot be fully freed from the emanations of this powerful substance. The sun's rays to a certain extent remove these emanations, but their dispersion into space also causes no small harm. Try to carry out a psychic energy experiment near a slaughterhouse and you will receive signs of acute madness, not to mention the entities which attach themselves to the exposed blood. Not without foundation has blood been called sacred.

There can thus be observed different kinds of people. It is possible to convince oneself particularly as to how strong atavism is. The desire for food containing blood is augmented by atavism, because the many preceding generations were saturated with blood. Unfortunately, governments pay no attention to improving the health of the population. State medicine and hygiene stand at a low level. Medical supervision is no higher than that of the police. No new thought penetrates into these outworn institutions. They can only prosecute, they cannot help.

Hence, on the path to Brotherhood there should be no slaughterhouses.

22. Yet there are people who speak much against bloodshed but are themselves not averse to eating meat. There are many contradictions contained in man. Only the perfecting of psychic energy can promote the harmonization of life. Contradiction is nothing but disorder. Different strata have corresponding contents. But a tempest can stir up waves, and not quickly thereafter is the right current again established.

23. We have spoken about the mixture of strata. In cosmic storms the current of chemism is constantly being unsettled and the rays refracted. It is not easy to assimilate such perturbations unless we remember about the inviolability of the laws. Astrology, remaining a science, can still undergo many fluctuations due to earthly lack of information. In addition, many signs have been concealed. We say this, not by way of disillusionment, but on the contrary, in order to remind observers about the complexity of conditions.

24. Hypocrisy, bigotry, and superstition are three of the dark qualities which must be rejected on the path to Brotherhood. Let each one reflect whence have been born these minions of ignorance. Whole books can be written about such paths of darkness. One should ponder upon how these pernicious corrupters have grown up. They grow imperceptibly. But there has never been a time when they were more numerous than at present. Notwithstanding the spiritualization of science, and in spite of conditions of rational investigation of the manifestations of the Subtle World, still

the growth of crimes due to ignorance is unprecedented. People cannot understand that spatial thought can free them from their shackles.

Consider the dark times as passing—knowledge shames the ignorant.

25. The pathway to Brotherhood is a high path. As a mountain is seen from afar, so, too, is Brotherhood. The Teacher cannot be insistent where the eyes are near-sighted. And during the ascent the outlines of the summit are lost from view. Right around it one does not distinguish the height, so, too, on the path to Brotherhood there are many turnings of the way. One should become accustomed to thought about the complexity of attainment. One should grow to love all the obstacles, for the stones on the path are but the steps of ascent. Long ago was it said that one does not ascend by a smooth stone.

26. Appeal to the Brotherhood does not remain without a response, but there are many ways of answering. People revolve so much within the circle of their own expressions that they do not perceive other signs. Besides, people are unable to understand the allusions and warnings that are sometimes contained in a single word and in a single spark. They do not wish to reflect about the reasons for such brevity. Scholars, even very erudite ones, do not remember the law of karma. Yet when people see a passer-by being exposed to danger, they warn him with a short outcry and do not read him lectures on the cause of his misfortune. So, too, in the matter of karmic reactions it is usually possible to caution with a brief exclamation without delving into the depths of karma.

Everyone has had opportunity many times to convince himself that the response of the Brotherhood has come in signs which are outwardly very insignificant. It can be boldly affirmed that a great majority of indications either glide over the consciousness or are incorrectly interpreted. Such distortions of the meaning are especially harmful when they are in the hands of thoughtless people who subject the indications to their own fortuitous frame of mind.

There are many instances when essential signs have been explained by the ignorant as something completely opposite. In their earthly customs people often interpret letters in their own way, not being concerned with the precise meaning of the words—such conventional egoistic practices have to be abandoned on the paths to Brotherhood.

27. By acting attentively in their earthly relations, people will accustom themselves also to attentiveness in the Higher Service. Do not leave the questions of people unanswered. It is better to reply as briefly as possible than to leave behind the engendering of poison. It can be easily shown what poisonous fermentations are begun where there is no link.

28. Enough is known about the existence of the Brotherhood of Good and the Brotherhood of Evil. It is likewise well known that the latter strives to imitate the former in the means and methods of action. The ignorant inquire, "Is it possible for man to distinguish, in the approach, this or that Brother?" If the appearance and words be identical, then it is not difficult to fall into error and to accept advices which lead to evil. Thus will reason the man who does not know that the means of discrimination are contained in the heart. The employment of psychic energy helps to discern infallibly the inner essence of the manifestations. No complicated devices are necessary when man bears within himself the spark of knowledge.

Investigators of psychic energy can bear witness

that the evidences of the energy are infallible. They can be relative in the matter of earthly dates, but in quality they will not be erroneous. And it is precisely quality that is necessary for discrimination of the essence. The primary energy cannot show the negative to be positive. Such purely scientific evidence protects people against an evil approach. Not without foundation is such discrimination called the armor of Light.

29. It may be asked why such a needed weapon is not entrusted to everyone. Each one does have it, but it is often closed up behind seven locks. People themselves are to blame that they lock up their greatest treasure in the cellar. Many, even after hearing about such energy, are not eager to learn about the means of its discovery—so undeveloped is love of knowledge!

30. The same awakened energy enables people to provide themselves with calmness in observing events. An investigator must not be irritated or agitated during observations. The manifestation of calmness will be a sign of Service. It is impossible to be devoted to Service if one's essence be billowing like waves under a cross wind.

31. The Teaching has already transformed your whole life. It has brought you through many dangers. The Teaching helps you to discriminate where harm is and where advantage. It does not come easily to distinguish the right pathway, but you know how to ascend a smooth rock. Psychic energy is developed from such tensions.

32. Psychic energy should be not only studied but consciously applied in life. Such a conscious cooperation as Brotherhood is in need of psychic energy. It is impossible to harmonize labor without psychic energy. It is impossible to arrive at mutual understanding without psychic energy. It is impossible to gather patience and tolerance without psychic energy. It is impossible to rid oneself from irritation without psychic energy. In everything there must be application of the primary energy itself.

It has already been observed that not only does the presence of an individual have an influence on the fluctuations of the energy but even pictures of people react upon the subtle energy. One must not only recognize the sensitiveness of the energy but also keep in mind this phenomenal quality. For people who have not seen experiments with psychic energy, discussions about the reactions even to images will seem like mad fairy tales. However, for such people as these, the energy itself is under suspicion. They are not averse to talking about spirit or soul, but this very obvious energy will be for them witchcraft.

33. One must learn not to irritate people to whom certain knowledge is inaccessible. Experienced observation whispers to one when discussion will be in vain.

34. It is possible for an argument to make the truth manifest, but most often it litters the space. The teacher must know to what extent the pupil can engage in argument without introducing irritation.

These measures must be known, because Brotherhood first of all needs equilibrium.

35. Be not surprised that, speaking about Brotherhood, I mention the primary energy; there are two reasons for this. The first lies in the fact that approach to Brotherhood requires the development of the primary energy. Without this, with the centers sleeping, realization of such subtle perceptions is impossible. On such most subtle vibrations is built Brotherly cooperation. The second thing to be remembered is that not everyone has read the preceding writings, in which psychic energy is spoken about. Each book must contain the basic conditions for improvement. It would be cruel not to give even brief allusions to the preceding, wherein something invaluable has been dealt with.

Let us be attentive to each small circumstance. In the earthly way of life it is difficult to distinguish where is the small and where the great, where the useless and where the useful. Many pearls have been swept away with the dust. If you notice that your companion is only partially assimilating vital principles, help him. In such patient assistance there is expressed a very important quality for brotherhood.

36. Psychic energy is called the organ of the fourth dimension. Indeed, the fact of this dimension is relative; it only expresses the refined state of all feelings. Great refinement bestows the possibility of understanding supermundane conditions. But if the fourth dimension has been established in the nomenclature, let it be thus—so long as we do not revert to two dimensions. Likewise, let us not object if psychic energy be called an organ. It exists, it produces powerful reactions. It assimilates cosmic currents, it is bound up with life. Let it be called even an organ, for in such designation there already is acknowledgment of it.

37. It must not be forgotten that, on the whole, many will not understand a single word about psychic energy. They will not accept it. Just as a man who has never seen lightning does not recognize it. Thus, there are to be found people who do not understand on the whole what thought is. The characteristic of such people will not be illiteracy but obduracy. Not few are such corpses!

Let investigators of psychic energy inure themselves to such petrifications. Much about an obvious inability to assimilate will have to be noted in the diaries.

38. People await Messengers, yet they are very

much frightened at a mere thought about their arrival. If one were to ask the people in what form they would like to see a Messenger, a strange conglomeration would emerge, even bordering upon the monstrous; bird feathers will not be last in their list of Messenger's attributes. And when people are told that the Messenger is surrounded by Light, they take precautions first of all not to be blinded.

True, there may occur shocks during even the most ordinary manifestations. A palpitation may be not from unexpectedness alone, it may arise from an inequality of auras. Such a tension can be even disastrous; therefore the appearance of Messengers does not occur frequently. Surely they come not to kill, consequently one must accustom oneself gradually to experiencing different tensions. Investigators of psychic energy will understand what exercise We are speaking about.

Besides experiments with psychic energy, it is necessary to accustom oneself to communion with the Subtle World—and without resorting to magic. Everything natural is to be attained by natural methods. Only by the way of experiment do people accustom themselves to tensions of various degrees. It may be understood that expectation itself will be a natural preparation, or discipline, as it is customary to say.

A man in a state of preparedness is ready to receive the Messenger.

39. People fear tests. They are afraid of experiments, but they cannot even imagine all the possible means of learning. Again physical fear, terror of the flesh, shackles rational actions. Therefore, in disciplinary training terror, first of all, has to be conquered.

40. The concept of Brotherhood stands on steadfast pillars. In it there can be no restrictions of age, race, or of occasional moods. Indeed, above all else there is the primary energy. If it is manifest, and if contacts through it can be harmonized, then there will be affirmed a lasting bond.

41. What is the natural path? The most unrestricted way of learning, with tolerance and patience, without any sectarianism. Unrestricted cognition is not easily adopted. Everything connected with human labors is limited. Every occupation cuts short, as it were, many ways of communion. Even excellent minds have been driven into a narrow channel. The disease of self-limitation bears no resemblance to self-sacrifice. Man limits himself for his own comfort. Indeed, bold actions for the sake of unrestricted knowledge will be the exception. Malice and hatred carry out their actions in straitness of mind. For unconfined action it is necessary for one to be filled with magnanimity and to discover causes and effects with a benevolent eye. Austerity of labor has nothing in common with a censorious attitude. Only limited people condemn. Not out of condemnation is perfectment born.

Is it possible to dream about unlimited knowledge when in confusion? One may learn everywhere and always. Possibilities themselves are attracted toward irrepressible striving. Only in motion lies the natural path!

42. Verily, one has to seek! One has to keep in mind that a small spark produces a great explosion. A single thought may both attract and repel. Those who rule human minds are often themselves being led. And what empty sounds can stifle the will of a man and forever impede the path already molded!

Good does not hinder, but evil does. Thus, let us remember that small sparks produce great explosions.

43. Are such preparations needed for Brotherhood? Definitely, not only preparation but also illumination. Will not he who decides to devote himself to the Great Service regret it? From faint-heartedness there will arise many thoughts about comfort and convenience. There may be even smiles of regret. How, then, to overcome such assaults without illumination?

44. Let us agree on the meaning of the concept of rest. Around this concept a multitude of false and harmful interpretations have clustered. People have become accustomed to think that rest is inaction; in this way it has become transformed into psychic enfeeblement. Inaction is most corruptive for psychic energy. Each spiritual immobility will fatigue, not regenerate.

Physicians prescribe rest, quiet, all kinds of inaction, and assume that in a moribund state it is possible to restore strength. But these same physicians understand that weakness and collapse result from violation of equilibrium. Thus, rest is nothing but equilibrium. But equilibrium is a proportionate tension of energy. Only thus is it possible to restore and strengthen one's forces.

It is of no consequence whether equilibrium be acquired in desert or city—the main requisite is constant tension. The path of tension is the path of striving, that is to say, the path of life.

The incompetent physician warns against expenditure of strength, but strength is dissipated through lack of equilibrium. Truly, then, equilibrium will be the best, the only panacea. A sensible use of fresh air is worthy of consideration as an assisting expedient, but this does not require a long period of time.

Let the concept of rest be rightly understood for the manifestation of Brotherhood. Unrest begets aimless bustle.

45. Among the universal manifestations, incessant explosions have a special significance. Likewise in man are there compressions and explosions of energy. But why are universal explosions beneficial, whereas the human ones can destroy the organism? The difference lies in the fact that universal explosions are balanced in a great rhythm, but the human ones often are devoid precisely of rhythm.

46. Everything is relative, but it is impossible to compare the harmony of the Universe with human free will. Precisely this bountiful gift, when not rightly used, imposes grave consequences. Much has been said about the significance of man in the Cosmos, but this truth must be reiterated unceasingly. One can become convinced as to how much people fail to think about their destination.

47. There was an ancient game in which people tried to make each other angry. Whoever became angry first was the loser.

48. Constant alertness is often indicated, but how seldom it is understood! Usually people will require it of those surrounding them, but they will not seek it in themselves. Whereas each one should attune first of all his own instrument. Only then is receptivity acquired. Is it possible to look forward to cooperation and Brotherhood without receptivity? The most definite counsels are broken against the armor of negation.

The time will come when physicians will discover what conditions are most advantageous for the action of psychic energy. One should not presume that psychic energy can act identically under all conditions. As there are people upon whom the most powerful poisons have no effect, psychic energy also is assimilated in different ways. If receptivity will not be developed, then man will lose his most precious apparatus. But for receptivity one must establish in oneself constant alertness. For such a quality nothing supernatural is required, one has only to be attentive.

49. Among one's human incarnations there is invariably found an incarnation devoted to rhythmic labor. Whether this be some sort of craftsmanship or music, singing or farm work, every man infallibly will cultivate in himself the rhythm which fills all of life. Upon learning of certain incarnations, people frequently are astonished as to why they should have been so insignificant. But in them there was being worked out the rhythm of labor. One of the greatest of qualities, this must be acquired through conflict and patience.

50. Growing to love work is possible only by cognizing it. Likewise, rhythm can be realized only when it has been absorbed into the nature of a man. Otherwise ignorance will rise up against lawful measures and constant discipline. To such ignorant ones the very concept of Brotherhood will appear as an intolerable utopia.

51. Brotherhood is a lofty expression of mutual human relations. In the state of Brotherhood one may reach a free realization of Hierarchy. Precisely, Hierarchy cannot be imposed. It lives only in voluntary realization. It cannot be accepted out of cunning considerations, for such a false situation ends in frightful dissolution. Recognition of Hierarchy will be accompanied by joy, but all coercion and falsehood is attended by grief.

Not so long ago one could have regarded such discussions as moral abstractions; but when psychic energy is evaluated then human qualities will become scientific values. Is the possibility not attractive to be able to establish a scale of qualities on an experimental basis?

52. It is incorrect to say that every growing plant is in rotary motion. It is more accurate to speak about spiral motion. Rotation is understood as something conclusive, whereas each turn cannot be final, since it is moving onward.

Such experiments can be carried out not only with plants but also with various projectiles; and eventually, when observing the flights of thought, it will be possible to convince oneself that all movement is spiral. In studying psychic energy such a consideration is useful.

53. Can Communications scientifically based be altered and become contradictory? Indeed, the fundamentals are steadfast, but there can be fluctuations in the receivers. Such manifestations of non-conformity should not be referred to the fundamentals. Is it not better to seek the cause in one's own lack of understanding? Only a broadened consciousness will help to establish a clear understanding, otherwise the most lucid letter can be misinterpreted.

Any instability is inadmissible.

54. Compare a delineation of manifestations of good will and gratitude with the hieroglyphs of malice and envy. In the first you will obtain a beautiful circle, while the second yields ugly scrawls. In spite of strong tension, malice produces disorderly lines. Such a disharmonious structure manifests abasement of all creative fundamentals. It is impossible to create by means of evil; it produces temporary convulsions, then it falls into madness and consumes itself.

But beautiful is the circle of magnanimity; it is as a shield of Light! It can expand and deepen in harmony of movement. In investigations of the primary energy it is instructive to convince oneself as to how clearly it has been granted man to distinguish positive and negative qualities. Already much has been repeated to people about the relativity of good and evil. But there is the basic impulse, which does not lead one into error; it is impossible to counterfeit the depictions of psychic energy, they indicate the essential nature of things.

55. It is impossible to doubt the tracings of psychic energy. As a primary force of cognition it cannot be misread by taking a casual mood for the essence. The manifestation of thought about the significance of psychic energy will be, as it were, a pumping of it from space.

The magnet of thought brings in most precious particles of psychic energy. One must grow to love it. One must recognize its constant presence. Such thinking is by no means easy. A great deal of patience must be found in order to protect it under the attack of all the unbridled currents of space.

56. Patience, patience, patience—let this not be an empty sound, let it protect one on all paths. When it seems that all forces have been exhausted, such an illusion is most dangerous. The forces are inexhaustible, but people themselves try to cut short their flow.

Also, the path to Brotherhood requires much patience. The same power of thought must be applied in order to draw close to the consciousness of the three worlds.

57. The true family is the prototype of communal life. It can personify cooperation and Hierarchy and all the conditions of Brotherhood. But such families are extremely rare, and therefore it is impossible to say to everyone that the family is the symbol of Brotherhood. It might be replied, "Is not the family a symbol of hostility?" So much have people become accustomed not to respect the home. Therefore, as to the question of upbringing, let us pay special attention to the life in the home. It is impossible to think about building the state without building the home.

What conception of Brotherhood can the people have who do not understand the dignity of state and home? No specific decree can restore the feeling of dignity if it has been obliterated. It is necessary to begin its implantation by education, by recognition of the value of broad knowledge and of exact scientific studies. Only thus can people again remember humaneness.

Upon the step of humaneness will the understanding of Brotherhood be established.

58. The very austerity of labor can acquire a beautiful meaning by the elimination of all coarsening effects and the introduction of the concept of cooperation. It must be remembered that coarseness is contrary to all laws of nature. Every coarse action creates such a hideous vortex that if people could but see it they would certainly be more careful in their conduct. The karma of coarseness is extremely heavy.

With broadening of consciousness people become especially sensitive to any and every coarseness. Thus, one may be assured that coarseness is most inadmissible.

59. Many listeners, no doubt, would prefer to hear sooner about Brotherhood itself; but let them first abandon curiosity and the obstructing habits. With dignity it is possible to enter. Therefore, it is first necessary to ascertain how different feelings are understood. One should not give precious things into someone's safekeeping if it is assumed that they will be resold instead of being carefully guarded.

He who wishes to learn will not weary of the path of cognition.

60. We strengthen our listeners with all the qualities necessary on the path to Brotherhood. It is not enough to possess only certain separate qualities, it is needful to realize their complete combination. The symphony of qualities is like the symphony of the spheres. If one quality develops beautifully while others are straggling, there results a destructive dissonance. Dissonance can be weakening or irritating, or even destructive. Equilibrium of qualities is achieved through great tension of consciousness. The shepherd must carefully tend his flock, and likewise man must cure an ailing quality. A man himself knows definitely which of his qualities is ailing. Life provides him with an opportunity to test any quality whatsoever. In everyday life there can be found the possibility of application of any quality. If a man begins to insist that he has been deprived of the possibility of applying his best qualities, he will reveal his own dullness. On the other hand, if a man rejoices at a chance to apply his qualities, he exhibits broadening of consciousness. Then comes the next step of joy, precisely that concerning the beauty of symphony of qualities.

61. Experiments with psychic energy will show how much such a symphony expands the beneficial circle. Experienced observers will apprehend easily the correlation of qualities with psychic energy, but for the ignorant such a comparison will be incomprehensible.

For the long journey let us gather together as many qualities as possible. Let each of them be of the best degree!

62. It must not be forgotten that each discovery is followed by discovery of its antithesis. You have heard how radio transmission has been interrupted over wide expanses; this means that even such a great discovery is not untrammelled. Some rays make objects invisible, and others pass through solid bodies. Only thought and psychic energy are absolutely untrammelled.

Humanity must select the most firm paths. All mechanical discoveries merely demonstrate the need of the power in man himself. Let us be solicitous toward everyone who can bring to humanity his best strength. And let us be grateful to the Brothers, who untiringly bring realization of psychic energy. On this path there has to be much selflessness. The ignorant cannot stand all the seekers of the immutable treasures. Robbery may be expected on the best path. Fortunately, the Bearers of the unseen treasures are invulnerable.

63. It has been said that virtue has a rainbow aura. The rainbow is the symbol of synthesis. Is not virtue revealed as a synthesis of qualities? In each ancient symbol can be found an unquestionable truth. People have understood that virtue is not simply the doing of good. They have distinctly known that only consonances of tensions of the best qualities provide the synthesis of ascent. They have known that only the motive will be the affirmation of virtue. No outward actions can testify to the intentions. Experiments with psychic energy will reveal to what extent action is to be distinguished from motive. No glittering words and actions can conceal intention. Many historical instances can be cited when, because of an unworthy motive, even useful actions could not be justified. On the other hand, much that remained inexplicable and under suspicion has shown the radiance of beautiful motives. Such evidences of the essence of life will be confirmed by the primary energy.

64. It must be understood that approach to such a lofty concept as Brotherhood imposes not an easy obligation. Each deliverance from a petty habit requires tension of the will. Furthermore, it may happen that a seemingly abandoned habit comes back again, and in a stronger degree; this means that this defect has continued to exist in the depths of the consciousness.

It may be asked, "Do habits linger on for several incarnations?" They can remain, and even grow, if the sojourn in the Subtle World has not been passed in the higher spheres. Everywhere motive has the decisive significance. Hence, at passage into the Subtle World the motive will be the conductor. Not the apparent but the heartfelt good intention will be beautiful, more beautiful than the most illustrious deeds. Only the man himself knows how this or that feeling has been engendered in him. He can inwardly follow the process of growth. Thus, the best judge is within oneself.

But let man remember that even in the earthly existence an impartial witness has been given—the primary energy.

65. Sternness and cruelty are quite different concepts. But people do not know how to distinguish the harmony of sternness from the spasms of cruelty. Sternness is an attribute of justice, but cruelty is misanthropy. From cruelty there is no path leading to Brotherhood. Sternness is expressed as a circle, but cruelty is the sign of madness. One should not understand cruelty as a disease; like foul speech, it is merely the expression of a base nature.

In the state, both these dark offshoots must be excluded by law. In primary schools there must be established the principles which will make clear the inadmissibility of these two most low defects.

66. Co-workers and messengers may be either conscious or unconscious ones. The entrusting of commissions is considered honorable, but unconscious co-workers usually do not even know when they have been inspired by a commission. They proceed in accord with a command unknown to them, transmitting something or forewarning someone, but they themselves do not know where is the beginning and where the end of their mission. There are many such messengers; they differ according to their condition, but none the less they do not tarry. Also, there are particular silent commissions, when it is needful to exert influence, not by a word, but by silence.

67. Sometimes a fixed silent gaze averts great dangers. Thought needs no words. Suggestion needs no words. Only unskillful hypnotists try to exert influence with a loud cry and to increase it with the hands, but neither one nor the other is needed in thought transmission. Rather can rhythmic breathing be useful, but this too is replaced by the rhythm of the heart.

Thought is sent through the heart and is also received through the heart.

68. People who are expecting a message can also be divided into two categories. The minority know how to wait, but the majority not only do not understand what is taking place but even exert a harmful influence. They abandon their work. They fill space with complaints. They impede those around them. Without noticing it they consider themselves the elect, and they begin to make arrogant assertions about others. Much harm emanates from scant knowledge and still more from a petrified consciousness. Each such person becomes a hotbed of confusion and doubt. He loses the rhythm of work by manifesting confusion. Such people are very harmful for the spreading of knowledge. They wish to receive for their personal gratification the very latest tidings, but little usefulness results from such usurpers. One should not take such weak people into account—they are as nests of treason. Nothing restrains their intrigues. There should be no act of destruction just for the sake of good tidings. Few there are who know how to await messages in complete magnanimity, while working, and amidst difficulties—such co-workers are the ones who become brothers.

69. One cannot accept everything written about the Brotherhood as authentic. Much has been confused with imaginings about the Subtle World; many personal dreams are interwoven with reality. There exist many legends about various races and non-existent continents. To a concept which attracts them, people attach many details without being concerned about their heterogeneity of kind and time. A poor imagination often belittles that which it wishes to glorify.

70. Right is the path from small to great. Each seed confirms this. But often people take the small for the great and think that a small coin can hide the sun.

71. A healer treats an ailment by incantation, but only recently are people beginning to understand that such incantations are, in fact, hypnotic suggestion. Healers appear to utter seemingly incomprehensible and meaningless words, but few reflect that the effectiveness is not in the meaning of such expressions but in the rhythm and, principally, in the thoughts being sent.

By means of suggestion it is possible not only to forestall pain, but even to give an entirely different direction to the illness. Rarely is the latter admitted, for up to the present time people have not believed much in the influence of thought. From the same source, from unbelief, comes stagnation of consciousness. People poison themselves by unbelief. The wisdom of ages has recorded many examples of great trust and also of destruction through mistrust. When We speak about cooperation and even about Brotherhood, We must repeat about trust—without it no rhythm is created, without it success is not invoked, without it there can be no advance. Do not think that I am reiterating something too generally known; on the contrary, as in an hour of danger I am repeating about the salutary expedient. There is no other way to awaken the psychic energy. There is no other path on which the heart can glow with victory. It is difficult not to weary if there be darkness in the heart.

72. One can receive the best counsels, and still they may remain as autumn leaves. Only the realization of the important use of the energy in life can bring effectively the Guidance. Empty words lead not to Brotherhood.

73. In the hour of confusion silence is the best friend. But let this quiet be not the stillness of malice. Though only momentarily, let the rhythm of the heart calm down. Let there be found again the quiet of psychic energy; thus will be strengthened the work of the centers—alight, but without inflammation.

74. "The city has been fully fortified, its walls and towers are strong, at each gate stands a sentry—no enemy can penetrate into the stronghold. However, sentinels, be wary, be not confounded by the arrows of the enemy. The arrows have been devised with special inscriptions for the purpose of distracting the attention of those on watch. The inscriptions are to allure the sentries, so that their minds will be confused and the gates will be left defenseless." Thus was described in a certain Mystery the state of psychic energy during the confusion of the spirit.

Whether expressed in poetic images, or in symbols, or in hieroglyphs, or in medical terms, or in a stern command—all forms will point identically to the significance of the basic energy. Often, in the Mysteries symbols cautioning against harmful confusion were employed. One may augment strongly the psychic energy, but even small confusion can open the gates to the most dangerous enemy. In an hour of consternation one must know how to evoke even a momentary calm. Such calmness and but one breath of prana will provide a strong shield.

The physician must harken attentively to the ancient symbols. When Biblical narratives speak about the visitation of illnesses and plagues, it may be understood that the depressed spirit had admitted the most frightful contagions.

75. It must be understood also that when one speaks about the good, right action is presupposed. If right action takes place, then good results from it. But if during the most brilliant talk about the good poor action is performed, then only harm will be created.

There is much talk about good and much evil is done.

76. People assume that a penny tossed to a beggar expiates a committed murder! So long as co-measurement is not realized, no equilibrium can result. Likewise, killing of spirit as well as of body is not understood. Where is the manifestation of Brotherhood, if murder of the spirit be possible? It is not even considered a crime!

77. Courage is increased by proper development of psychic energy. Proper development must be understood as natural growth. Let each one augment his store of courage; it is like opening a window.

78. Destructive is the feeling of contentment. It leads to satiation and to paralysis of energy. One may observe in the Subtle World the most pitiful fate of such paralytics. Even the little that they have succeeded in accumulating during their earthly life is cut

short by paralysis of energy. Vagrant shades, they cannot succeed, because without energy it is impossible to advance. You may be asked whose lot is more gloomy, that of such paralytics or of the malignant haters. The answer is difficult. Those who hate can suffer and thus be purified, but through disuse of energy the paralytics lose the possibility of advancing. Is it not better to suffer much but with the possibility of advance? The torments that purify are better than hopeless dissolution. Hatred can be transformed into love, but paralysis is the terror of night. Such hopeless destructions cannot lead to Brotherhood. Paralysis of separate limbs can be overcome by the will, but if the basic energy itself is inactive how can a command be carried out? Many such living corpses walk about!

79. It is useful to observe how people act under suggestion, but at the same time violently deny the possibility of such an influence. Sometimes, out of malice, a man asserts that his conduct is in accord with his own intentions, whereas he is acting under direct suggestion. Man transmits thoughts which are not his own, and makes use of expressions which are alien to him, but because of malice he tries to ascribe them to himself. If one knows whence a suggestion has issued, one can form an opinion about an intentional distortion.

Dark and unsteady is everything created by malice.

80. Usually, when people return to a former place they experience a certain sadness. They feel that something has not been accomplished. And so it is. In Infinity there must always be sensed something preordained.

81. The book about Brotherhood will be divided into two parts. The first, about the foundations of Brotherhood, will be given now; the second, about the inner life of the Brotherhood, We shall send to those who will accept the foundations.

82. Composite dreams and recollections represent in themselves a whole science. Sometimes they weave themselves into tall tales, but upon dissection they manifest a whole series of separate episodes which are quite real. Therefore, when people speak about something as being impossible, one should reflect that perhaps a combination of some parts may be unnatural, whereas each one of them may be entirely possible. It is instructive to observe precisely which parts of recollections fall out more easily; thus the character of the person himself can be elucidated.

The manifestation of the most remote recollections can create complex patterns from different epochs. The most heterogeneous encounters can be perceived. Thus, oftentimes Brothers could have been encountered, but even the loftiest contacts could be obscured by details out of the various ages. Not without reason has it been said that every man represents in himself a complicated repository. Much fire is needed in order to illumine all the dark storehouses.

83. People talk much about thought-forms, but not all thoughts can be clothed in a form. There can be mental dust, which not only has been deprived of formation but which is intermingling with other similar dust clouds. One may begin to sneeze from such rubbish.

84. Those who talk about thought-forms are rarely concerned with refining and strengthening these formations. But even autosuggestion can be useful. Long ago was it said that thoughts are borne in space; hence, it is a premise that they must be formed. Clouds of dusty rubbish are not suitable for sending.

85. The bliss of the thinker or the torment of the

thinker? It is customary to represent a thinker as in torment, but if you ask him whether he wishes to be freed from such pangs, any thinker will reply in the negative. In the depth of his consciousness he experiences great bliss, for the process of thinking is a higher enjoyment. People have only two real joys—thinking and the ecstasy over beauty. The path to the Fiery World has been affirmed by these two manifestations. Only through them can man advance to the lofty spheres. Every higher communion will contain these two fundamentals. Therefore, it is absurd to talk about the torments of the thinker or the creator. They are not suffering but rejoicing. However, people understand joy in such a singular fashion! For some people joy is in thinking nothing and doing nothing.

The path to Brotherhood is in thinking and in labor.

86. Mercy is not an easy concept, and only the very far-sighted can scrutinize the effects of it. When magnanimity prompts, "Let live!" this verdict will not be difficult. Perhaps, precisely in this hour destruction might have been approaching, but the far-sighted one understood that the positive is greater than the negative. For the near-sighted such mercy is unfitting, but for the far-sighted it is as an arrow into the target.

87. There are many signs on the path to Brotherhood. The path is not a short one, and all provisions are useful. Who dares to affirm that this or that quality is not suitable for him? It may turn out that precisely the most neglected will be urgently needed.

88. The Burden of this World. Two disciples were discussing the most expressive symbol for this concept. One proposed gold, but the other suggested that white marble might be better. Both agreed that a burden, meaning something weighty, would best be expressed by a stone. But the Teacher observed, "The smallest seed corresponds to the concept of the burden of the world."

89. Do not tell much about the far-off worlds to people who in their earthly existence are unable to understand their own destination. They will lose that little bit of their own, and will not acquire anything useful from the realm of higher knowledge. Observe very attentively what can be contained by a man. People do not begin dinner with a dessert. It is especially harmful to feed people with indigestible food. The more so is it essential to develop attentiveness within oneself. Listeners must not be bored, for boredom is stagnation.

90. People willingly aspire to a Brotherhood with a ready-made form. But if they are forewarned that quarreling is not permitted, a substantial number of them will lose their enthusiasm.

Ask people how they picture the Brotherhood. You will find many minor conditions that seem especially important to them. One inquirer was amazed and finally exclaimed, "Can disorder be so esteemed by people!"

Verily, they do not know about the immutable laws of nature.

91. In the most difficult hour people can still occupy themselves with ordinary matters. It is amazing how often a lack of understanding of events is revealed. Repetition about the importance of the hour is not effective. Realization does not knock at the heart. Let us not wait for previsions, however a premonition is entirely natural. Yet people reject these premonitions because no one has told them about the primary energy. Thus people succeed in one thing, but retreat in another no less precious.

92. Detested labor is not only a misery for the

unsuccessful worker but it poisons the whole surrounding atmosphere. The discontent of the worker does not permit him to find joy and to improve the quality. Moreover, imperil born of irritation redoubles gloomy thoughts, with effects fatal to creativeness. But the definite question may arise as to what is to be done if not everyone can find work corresponding to his vocation. Undoubtedly, many people cannot apply themselves in the way they would like. There exists a remedy for lifting such a blight. Scientific attainments show that above the everyday routine there is a beautiful domain accessible to all—the realization of psychic energy. In experiments with it one may be convinced that farmers often possess a goodly store of the energy. Likewise, many other fields of labor aid the conservation of energy. Therefore, amid the most diverse labors one may find uplifting strength.

93. All is possible; only depression of spirit can whisper about impossibility. Each step of science does not limit; it provides a new possibility. If something appears impossible from the earthly point of view, it may be entirely feasible through application of subtle energies. The face of a man changes with the source of light. Lighting can alter to the point of non-recognition the facial features and can reveal a quite unusual expression. But there are so many rays and currents, of diverse influence, and they can transform that which exists!

Is it not encouraging to realize that all is possible?

94. It is a sad situation if one is not subjected to attacks. This means that one's energy is in a very weak state and does not provoke any counteractions. Only the unenlightened consider attacks as misfortune. Obesity swims in the fat of inaction. For what sort of fertilization is such fat of use? The emanations of fat attract undesirable entities. More useful is alert striving; it preserves an adequate covering for the nerves. Likewise, thinness must not exceed the point of equilibrium.

95. Each manifestation is multiform. It is especially erroneous to think of a manifestation as having one single source and one single effect. Around each action there can be observed many different realms which exert an influence and on which an influence is exerted. One must assimilate the fact that the sphere of each action is far broader than can be defined according to earthly reasoning. Thus, by each action and each thought people contact several spheres. It should not be forgotten that thoughts infallibly impinge upon the Subtle World. They do not always arrive in a state of clarity, but in any case they will produce a certain disturbance of energy. So many currents are refracted in space that it is impossible to call human action a mere muscular reflex. Hence, one must accustom oneself to the complexity of effects.

96. Once there was an artist who wished to depict thought, but did not know what symbol would be best to express it. One philosopher suggested the conception of a cloud formation, because thought dwells in space. Another thinker believed that a starry heaven would be better. A third suggested that lightning would provide an austere representation of thought. A fourth proposed the idea of leaving the canvas blank, inasmuch as earthly eyes cannot catch a thought, and any form would be too crude for the light of the energy.

97. The starry heaven best of all can lead one away from earthly conditions. The manifestation of Infinity can overshadow earthly heaped-up piles. Earthly terror is eliminated only by the radiance of the far-off worlds.

98. Do not jump to conclusions. People usually rush prematurely and thus entangle the threads of effects.

99. Brotherhood or cooperation? It is impossible to define a sharp boundary between them. Whereas, people are desirous that concepts be quite sharply divided. But much flows into each concept from other concepts. Thus, cooperation will be, as it were, the threshold to Brotherhood; therefore, one must guard the approaches to the Stronghold of the Spirit.

100. The collapse of home and family will be, not in words and actions, but in thoughts. Silently are the foundations undermined. Without noticing it, people themselves foment dissolution. There are not many hearths around which mutual labor is performed in full understanding. But each such home is a step toward Brotherhood.

101. A groom expressed to his master a desire to breed a particular strain of horses. The master replied, "Your plan is excellent, but first put the stable in order." A writer is highly appreciative when his thoughts bring benefit and are not read lightly and fleetingly. Many examples may be cited from different domains to remind one about service, which is orderly in essence. That same orderliness must be applied when the thought about Brotherhood is being molded.

102. We should count each hour in which we have succeeded in expending our efforts in the accomplishment of our task. Service is not in furthering ordinary felicity but in bringing benefit to humanity. It may be difficult to admit individual personalities, but the face of all humanity will be acceptable.

103. How to reconcile the existence of free will with the influences about which much has been said? Free will does exist, and no one will deny it, yet one may constantly observe certain non-conformities with the actions and thoughts of the Supermundane Forces. The point is that the will may be harmonious with the Higher Forces, or it may be chaotic and working against construction. It is deplorable that the chaotic will predominates among people. It does not improve with formal education. Freedom of will is a prerogative of man, but without harmony with the Higher Forces it becomes a misfortune.

104. Though the harm of lower psychism has been spoken about often, still the ignorant cannot distinguish this state from the natural growth of the primary energy. If we hear about a confusing of lower psychism with psychic energy, we shall know that it would be useless, when encountering such ignorance, to try to persuade to the contrary. One should sense where the Source is which saturates our store of energy. One must esteem this Treasure.

105. In ancient treatises can be found the expression "crippled souls." And it is explained that such crippling can be done only by oneself. As soon as a man imagines that no further path remains for him, he shackles his own primary energy. In such fetters there can be no advance. By cutting short the path, the man takes upon himself a grave responsibility. This cannot be justified by despair, for of course this dark phantom is engendered by one's own weak will. Having lodged in the spirit, this specter actually injures the health. The phantom has nothing in it of reality. If people will investigate the true causes of despair, the invalidity of these causes will become amazingly clear. If the concept of Brotherhood were near to people, how many such groundless despairs would be dispelled! Yet people would rather cut short their own progress than reflect about the healing fundamentals. The writers of the ancient treatises about crippled souls had good grounds for this expression.

106. In every craft one may be convinced as to how difficult it is to guide in the presence of a hostile will. Not only an inimical but even an inert will can be injurious. Many possibilities already molded will be denied by an evil will. Not only in great events but throughout the entire structure of life can such a situation be observed.

107. Frequently a denier will affirm that he exerts no influence. And in such a case Brotherhood can be enormously useful. It is possible to approach a human being in an unusual way with the call of Brotherhood. As a physician, Brotherhood can have an effect upon the hostile will. However, for this the concept of Brotherhood must be assimilated. Do we often see this?

108. Is it possible to name a man who would be satisfied at receiving only half a garment instead of the whole one expected by him? And so it is in cooperation. If instead of a full brotherly collaboration half of what is offered is suspicion and doubt, then what kind of success can be achieved? It is needful to cultivate one's capacity for cooperation, beginning with the most routine tasks. It is a mistake to assume that cooperation is manifest in great deeds if it has not been present even in everyday ones. One should look deeply into the depths of one's consciousness and ask oneself whether the spirit is prepared for cooperation.

It is impossible for a man even to think about Brotherhood if he is not happy to take part in a common work. Each common work contains many aspects which correspond to different capabilities. Is the field of labor narrow? Is it not joyous to perceive true co-workers around oneself? The joy We feel at each co-worker is not small. It is necessary to encourage discreetly each one who draws near. But one need not lament those who fall by the wayside, if their spirit cannot understand true joy.

109. In Infinity there are many sensations that are inexpressible in earthly words. Some of them fill the heart with palpitation, yet such tension will be neither terror nor rapture. It is difficult to describe the feeling of the one who stands before the fathomless abyss. He is not frightened, yet he cannot act boldly. He does not see any support and he does not know what is to be done in such a situation. But it is his good fortune if behind him stands Brotherhood, completely realized. One should not understand Brotherhood as something abstract. It is here present for the happiness of humanity.

110. If the surpassing feeling of Brotherhood is difficult in the earthly condition, nevertheless Brotherhood is entirely accessible to each aspiring mind. There is no need to make something complicated of it, if you are able to wish for your neighbor nothing that you do not wish for yourself. Thus, every day, in every task, in every thought, one may be affirmed in the realization of Brotherhood.

111. Good deeds are like different flowers in a meadow. Among the healing ones there may be others which are quite brilliant but poisonous. Among the wonderful manifestations there may be found extremely deadly ones, but only by experiment is it possible to make a just selection. Insincerity contains a destructive poison. It can be observed that a construction built upon falsehood degenerates into hideousness. Much is being spoken about good deeds, but they must be truly good. Let people search the depths of their hearts as to when they have been good. No mask can conceal the ugliness of a skeleton of falsehood. Let us not condemn, for each one has already condemned himself.

112. Never has a tree cleft by lightning grown back together. It is impossible to penetrate into the depths of the heart if it has been darkened as by a lightning stroke. It is not to be expected that the burned tree will become strong and shady again. So, too, amidst calls to Brotherhood one should not rely upon a heart which has forgotten about good.

113. Any scientific knowledge is beautiful so far that it does not terminate in an impasse. A true seeker for knowledge recognizes no situation as issueless. He can gather constantly by developing new branches of cognition. For manifestations of preparedness for Brotherhood, such an infinitude of knowledge is the best step. It is not very easy to cognize such infinitude, yet for one who knows the trend of evolution it will be the natural and only path. But do not let the heart grow hard in such premises. Let rapture be preserved at each approach to new consciousness. A hardened heart will not ascend to the Tower. It will not give strength to the subtle body. Such a stony heart will remain within the confines of Earth. It is very important to understand the life of the heart. One should not permit it to revert to primeval stone. One should watch over the manifestations of the heart. Without it Brotherhood cannot be built.

114. Let us also not forget another quality indispensable on the path—non-attachment to property. Avarice in general is nowhere fitting; this quality holds one back to the lower spheres. The attachment of a miser is an insurmountable obstacle. While it is not easy to renounce property, avarice is indeed the most grave condition of plunging into the abyss.

115. One may make the mistake of assuming that

the majority of people know how to read books. Such ability has to be cultivated. When people accept the book, it does not mean that they know how to read it properly. It can be seen how relatively they interpret what has been read, and how far removed their understanding often is from the writer's thought. I affirm that books are too little comprehended, yet the manifestation of the primary energy can be an excellent guide. It frequently helps one to find a needed book and to select from it what is desired. One has but to be attentive. But this quality also must be cultivated in oneself.

116. Often one may hear narratives about the start or abolishment of the Brotherhood. Various countries are pointed out, many epochs are named, but no one can say authentically when Communities have been founded. People regard as a beautiful tale the remnants of indications about the Brotherhood. Many disputes, many misunderstandings are caused by the details about the structure of the earthly Brotherhood. Most often it is regarded in general as non-existent. It may be noticed that people fall into particular irritation in discussing the structure of the Brotherhood. Especially suspicious are people who do not admit the existence of anything higher than their imagination. They forget that the imagination is an accumulation of actuality. Hence, they cannot admit that there is anything above and beyond their own conception of life.

Too few are the travelers who pay attention to extraordinary manifestations. On the contrary, frequently the most exceptional evidences are dismissed by the most trivial explanations. People, as if blind, are unwilling to observe the evidence; they hasten away from it in order to shut themselves up in their conventional illusions. It may be asked, "Who then is more devoted to truth, he who sinks into the narcosis of illusion or he who is ready to encounter reality with keenness and courage?"

We esteem devotees of reality.

117. Let us not regard the skeptics as devotees of reality. Skeptics go through life muffled in a grey veil. They think that they are rebelling against illusion, but they cover themselves constantly with cobweb. Those people must be singled out who from early childhood have loved the truth.

118. In legends about Armageddon there are mentioned people with covered faces. Is there not something similar taking place now? It can be seen that the whole world is gradually putting on a veil and brother rises against brother. Precisely, the covered faces are marking time.

119. It may be noticed that patience is developed to the extreme in certain people while others are totally lacking in this quality. What is the reason for this? Such a basic quality cannot be a matter of chance. Know that the possessor of patience has built it up in many lives. A patient man is a worker of vast experience. Only in great labors does a man cognize the worthlessness of irritation. Before the Great Image he perceives the complete insignificance of transitory manifestations. Without many testings it is impossible to appraise and distinguish the qualities of manifestations in life. One should not assume that patience is a distinction conferred without reason; on the contrary, it belongs to the qualities that have been earned with special difficulty, both in the earthly and in the subtle sojourn. Hence, the patient man is rich in experience while the impatient one is a novice in life. Thus let us remember, for the Path.

120. Independence of action is an indispensable

quality. It is likewise not easily acquired. It may slip into arbitrariness or weaken to the point of dissolution. Every Teacher exerts his efforts to instill effective independent activity in the disciple, but how is one to reconcile this with Hierarchy? There are many misinterpretations impeding the encompassing of this concept. Whole treatises can be written about the contradiction between independent action and Hierarchy. There will be found very cunning whisperers who will try to prove that in this manner the immutability of Hierarchy is being shaken. The whisperers will try to conceal the fact that the independent action must be accompanied by attunement, or, as is said, by harmony, with all the degrees of consciousness.

121. One should know how to conquer the illusion of contradictions. It is needful on the one hand to cultivate kindheartedness and on the other to understand austerity. For many, such a task is completely insoluble; only the heart can prompt when the two qualities will not contradict each other. The heart will prompt when it is necessary to rush to the help of one's neighbor. The heart will indicate when to stop short the madness of a fierce animal. It is impossible to express in a word of law just when the necessity of this or that action becomes evident. Unwritten are the laws of the heart, but only therein does justice dwell, for the heart is the bridge of the worlds.

Where are the scales of self-abnegation? Where is the judge of achievement? Where is the measure of duty? The sword of knowledge flashes at the command of the heart. For the heart there will be no contradiction.

122. Penetration into the spheres of the Subtle World will not contradict earthly life. The life of the Subtle World is not necromancy; one must become

accustomed to the right understanding. If the earthly eyes do not yet see, nor the ears hear, still the heart does recognize reality. For progress, one needs to recognize the Supermundane World. Such a broadened consciousness will transform the entire attitude toward life. The time has drawn near when one must prepare the consciousness for broad perceptions. Only in a broad understanding will it be possible to discern the process that is taking place.

123. You see that the world is in a state of war. Diverse are its aspects! In one place they are concealed and in another they are obvious, but their meaning is one. Likewise, revolution takes on a peculiar meaning; it can also occur without this name. Some may think that the process is too slow, but in essence it is even hurried.

124. Many times has the planet been threatened with danger from comets. But even in the tensity of the atmosphere people have not sensed anything unusual. There have been certain individuals who understood how tensed the atmosphere was, but the great majority completely failed to notice anything. It is possible to carry out a curious experiment, observing how much humanity responds to certain events. It should be noticed that even conspicuous world events often do not reach the consciousness. The reason is that people wish to see things in their own way and do not permit their consciousness to express itself justly. Such people are not suited for cooperation.

125. Likewise, of little use are those who work in halfwayness. They are easily disappointed and obtain no results. Labor must be built upon complete devotion. Often it is not given to one to see the fruits of his work, but one must know that each drop of labor is already an indisputable acquisition. Such knowledge will permit prolongation of the work in the Subtle World also. Is it not all the same, if the task is fulfilled mentally and is impressed in thought-forms? The only condition is that the work be useful. It is not up to us to judge where labor is of the greatest usefulness; it has its own spiral.

126. Never before have we held discourses under such tension. Never has Earth been so enshrouded in brown gas. Never has the planet been so flooded with hatred. It is unthinkable not to sense the convulsions of nations; therefore, when I speak about care toward health I have in mind the unusual state of affairs throughout the world. It is regrettable that the nations do not think about the condition of the world. Much energy is being wasted. Do not think that the special tension comes only from private circumstances; it vibrates in conformity with the conditions in the world. The psychic energy is tensed, ready for both reception and repulsion. The spirit senses thoughts manifested in the Subtle World.

127. The explosions of stars have a significance for Earth, not at the moment of explosion, but when the photochemism produces its reactions. This example is also quite instructive for human relations. It is impossible to trace the beginning and ending of the boundary line of manifested correlations. Since there are heavenly bodies in the Universe which are far removed from each other yet have strong mutual reactions, then human fluids also can be active at remote distances. And between the dense world and the Subtle World one may thus perceive a most complex web of interaction. I am not speaking here about thought transmission, but about the emanation of fluids which, as a constant outflowing of primary energy, is impelled in accordance with the magnetic principle. This basis should be kept in mind during each cooperation.

128. It is customary to represent the manifested by a circle, assuming outside of it something unmanifested. Such a symbol is conditional, because the boundary line of the unmanifested is quite tortuous. It penetrates wherever resistance becomes weak.

129. It is futile to think that chaos is somewhere faraway; it is admitted by humanity during all disorderly thinking. Only a steadfast consciousness can be a protection against chaos. Sometimes the smallest outward manifestations come from most deep-seated concessions. The effect may result not only from malice, but also from decomposing chaos—quite a dangerous quality during cooperation.

130. "Brotherhood on Earth is impossible!" Thus exclaim those filled with selfhood. "Brotherhood on Earth is impossible," say the dark destroyers. "Brotherhood on Earth is impossible," whisper the weak-willed. Thus do many voices try to deny the fundamentals of Be-ness. Yet, so many true Brotherhoods have existed in different epochs, and nothing was able to cut short their existence. If people do not see something, then for them it does not exist. Such ignorance can be traced from ancient times up to this day. Nothing can force a man to see if he does not wish to see. It is time to understand that it is not only the visible that exists but that the world is filled with invisible realities.

131. Through what means can Brothers be in contact? If in the earthly body, then such connection will be a fleeting one. If in the subtle body, then, too, such unity may be frail. Only the bodies of Light can be mutually affirmed. Only under the one ray of the focal point is it possible to find mutual understanding. Thus, let us not consider the concept of Brotherhood superficially, as then it will remain within earthly bounds and will be useless. The guiding magnet is encompassed not in the earthly body, nor in the subtle, but in the seed of the spirit, in the given Light which surpasses imagination. He who does not understand the higher mystery of Brotherhood had better not belittle this concept. Let him plunge once again into the Subtle World and learn about the radiance of the Higher World. Perhaps the wayfarer will carry along a spark of Light in his new ascent?

Thus, let us adopt care toward the concept of Brotherhood.

132. A reflection is clear on a calm surface. Each agitation distorts the clarity. Likewise, the primary energy requires calmness in order to reflect Truth. It should not be assumed that calmness is decline and enfeeblement. Only disorderly agitation can distort the mirror of energy.

People talk much about the tranquillity of wise men, but it is really a great tension, so great that the surface of the energy becomes mirror-like. Thus, calmness must not be taken for inaction.

133. Defamation by the dark ones is praise. One may follow how the jinn helped to build temples. They did not suspect how much of their work was utilizable. A book could be written about the "Labors of the Jinn."

134. People who bear within themselves the element of brotherly cooperation can be observed from early childhood. Usually they are sharply distinguished from all surrounding them. Their power of observation is high and their impressionability strong. They are not satisfied with mediocrity and they stand apart, eschewing commonly accepted enjoyments. It can be observed that they seem to bear within themselves some sort of inner task. They can see much and make note of it in their consciousness. They are usually compassionate, as if they remember the value of this quality. They are indignant at grossness of conduct, as if realizing all the baseness of such quality. They are concentrated upon their favorite subjects, and they are surrounded by envy and malevolence, since they are not understood and remain alien among people. It is not easy to live one's life with an uplifted consciousness, as it cannot be content amidst the general denial of everything that leads toward Light.

Such chosen ones are not often encountered. Often they are unrecognized. Theirs is a dream which comes from afar, and which for other people will sometimes seem to border upon madness. From antiquity there has come the term "sacred madness." Wisdom is frequently spoken of as madness. Likewise do people refer to an uplifted consciousness. Let us not regard these as axioms generally known, for actually they remain neglected for entire ages.

Thus, the concept of Brotherhood enters the consciousness with difficulty.

135. The twilight of spirit is engendered by people themselves. The heritage of the Subtle World remains no more real than a dream. It even meets with the hostility of the reason. The reason does not accept manifestations of the Higher World. Especially burdensome for it is the fiery radiance.

136. Knowing how to deal with people according to their consciousness is a lofty quality. One should not forget that the majority of misfortunes proceed from a lack of such commensurateness. It is impossible to propose even very excellent things if they are above someone's consciousness. It is inadvisable to speak to an unprepared man about harmony or vibrational combinations. Who can foresee what such a man will visualize under the concepts of harmony or vibrational combinations? But he can understand it if told about carefulness toward his surroundings. The simplest concept concerning solicitude will be a firm basis for each cooperation of Brotherhood. It is desirable that every cooperation be a nursery of care. In this is expressed also attentiveness, solicitude, compassion, and love itself. How much strength may be conserved by care alone! So many cosmic reactions of the spirit may be regulated upon the use of the most simple care. It is impossible even to imagine to what an extent the aura of the home is strengthened where solicitude is definitely maintained. In many people the understanding of Hierarchy is completely obscured, but even in such cases solicitude will help to set the situation right—merely by being solicitous toward each other! This is no great obligation, and yet it is like a cornerstone.

137. People talk much about culture, but this fundamental too must not be made complicated. It is necessary to understand more simply the betterment of life and the raising of morality. Each one who is aware of a better life will regard with care everything beautiful. It is necessary to be more good.

138. Attentiveness helps one to take note of many external influences, but even this striving is developed by long experience.

139. Let us compare the quantity of mental achievements with those accomplished in earthly action. It is surprising to compare the number of mental solutions with the small quantity of manifested actions. Indeed, each thought directed toward good represents an unquestionable value. However it is instructive to trace how difficult the transmission of thought into earthly action has been made. One may truly be amazed as to why thoughts have been so far removed from action!

A strong enough thought needs no enlistment of action, but aside from such solitary thinkers there are a great number of thoughts which are good yet are not strong enough to react mentally and therefore do not reach the point of earthly action. As always, such a middle way is inert. It can impede the wholesome progress of man.

Thus, let us very solicitously render assistance, so that each germ of good thought be translated into action.

140. Each ascent is symbolized by action, but it is not easy to judge which action will conform to the thought. Many side issues will impede, coloring in their own way the attempts at action. One must have enormous patience and observation in order to be discriminating in the jungles of contradictions due to chaos. One has to love one's work in order to find therein rest and justification.

141. It may be asked, "Will the number of physicians decrease because of the increase of patent medicines?" This would be a calamity. Physicians are widely needed, if by the word physician one means a highly educated friend of humanity. Verily, the conventionally prepared remedies may bring on illnesses which will have to be treated individually in each case by the physician. There will be required a very subtle combination of suggestion together with the medicaments. We are not speaking about surgery, for this field calls for no discussion if it is kept within its proper limits. A surgeon who performs a needless operation is frequently likened to a murderer. Therefore, in this field also the true straight-knowledge is required.

Still more difficult is the problem of the physician

when there is a complication of several ailments; such cases are on the increase. It is possible to treat one disease and in so doing make another one worse. Even now there are many localities which are lacking in proper medical service. This situation results in a general lowering of vitality. Degeneration is not an imaginary thing. Everywhere there can be observed the signs of such disaster. Not only does this calamity strike down the present generation; it also corrupts the humanity of the future. The cry will be raised that such advice is old. But if so, why has it not been applied before this?

The manifestation of Brotherhood can flourish under conditions of true health.

142. Do not lead away to the distant planets people who are wavering. They will stumble because of ignorance. Let them first fortify the consciousness through lessons on Earth. Let them learn about cooperation, about trust, about discipline. A useful assignment concerning the betterment of life can be given to people. Let us not cut short the people's tasks, which would only lead them into new confusion. It is not the exceptions that need to be taken into account but the multitudes. Therefore, let us give at first the most undeferrable. What sort of Brotherhood could there be without the foundations?

143. Tatters are complicating the fundamentals of Be-ness. It is necessary to find the link between the earthly world and the Subtle World. Not on paper but in the heart is it necessary to know just what the people need. Worries and torments denote many mistakes. They arise from the fact that someone had in mind only one group, but not the people as a whole. Salutary counsels are needed for the people.

144. The farmer prepares and improves the field,

sows it in good time, and patiently awaits the sprouting and the harvest. He puts a fence around the field, so that animals may not trample down the young growth. Every farmer knows causes and effects. But it is not thus in human interrelations; people wish to know neither causes nor effects. They are not concerned about sprouts, and they want everything to be accomplished in their own arbitrarily prescribed way. Notwithstanding all the examples, people do doubt the cosmic law. They quite readily sow the causes, but they will not reflect that weeds may be the sole harvest.

Discourses about causes and effects should be introduced in the schools. Let the teacher propose a cause and the pupils think out the effects. In such conversations there will be displayed also the qualities of the students. It is possible to imagine many effects from one cause. Only a broadened consciousness will apprehend what effects will correspond to all the attendant circumstances. One should not be consoled by the fact that even a simple farmer can calculate a harvest. The manifestation of cosmic currents and of mental conflicts is far more complicated. From childhood on, let youth be accustomed to complicated effects and to dependence upon spatial thoughts. It should not be supposed that children need to have safeguards erected against their thinking.

145. People know more than they think they do. They hear about life on distant worlds. They know about energies and currents. They are in contact with many manifestations of nature. The question is merely as to how well they absorb all this information. During an accelerated accumulation of discoveries, it is especially needful to purify the consciousness. The moral foundations become, or rather should become, an attribute of knowledge; otherwise, the gulf between knowledge and morals widens dangerously.

146. Many sowings will sprout in a year's time. The essence of Armageddon lies not only in the exhaustion of old causes but also in the establishment of new ones. It is correct to call to mind what was indicated ten years ago. The causes have begun to give rise to effects. Perhaps someone did rashly utter some decisive word, and over a period of ten years it has resulted in either flame or water. Thus does thought work.

147. It is impossible to exclude from the rainbow even one single tint. Likewise, it is impossible to take away one single link from the Teaching of Life. The rainbow manifests a full spectrum, and the complete Teaching of Life likewise equips for the journey on all paths. The traveler is equally concerned about cloak and headdress and footwear. No one will say that he prefers hat to shoes or vice-versa. Therefore, when someone prefers one portion of the Teaching, he is acting like a traveler who has forgotten his shoes.

It may be that certain objects appear to be unnecessary at some given hour, whereas tomorrow precisely these may make the journey easier. There are to be found people to whom the simplest word proves to be the best key. It is impossible to visualize the great diversity of human consciousnesses. It were better that those who know be bored for a while than that someone be forever repulsed. New approaches to perfectment are unexpected, and new co-workers are not easily recognized.

148. People are vainly seeking new remedies and medicaments without making use of the old ones. Even milk and honey are not sufficiently in use. Whereas, what can be more beneficial than vegetable products reworked through a succeeding evolution? Milk and honey are to be had in infinite variety, and they constitute the best prophylaxis when employed rationally and scientifically. The point is not simply to drink milk and eat honey; first of all, one must consider what kind of milk and what kind of honey. It is right to assume that the best honey will be from places that are replete with curative herbs. It may be understood that bees bring together not mere chance combinations of their extractions. Nature lore about bees has importance in the way of directing attention to the particular quality of the honey.

Moreover, many vegetable products require investigation. People regard things so primitively that they are content with the expressions "good and bad," "fresh and spoiled;" besides, they are elated by the large size of a product, forgetting that artificial enlargement diminishes the qualitative value. Even such primitive considerations are lost sight of. In the development of vitality, its essence ought to be derived from all the kingdoms of nature.

149. Continuity is one of the basic qualities of the subtlest energies. People can take example from the higher worlds for earthly existence also. If it is difficult to maintain continuity in work, it can be fully realized in spiritual strivings. We, wayfarers of Earth, can form a link with the higher worlds in spirit; such a bond will permit us to dwell in close union with the invisible worlds. Such unity will teach also earthly unity. Beginning with the higher, let us also be affirmed in the lower. It is not easy to maintain earthly unity. Many petty circumstances intrude and blot out good intentions. Only the testing of forces in a higher application can create continuity of intercourse with the Higher World. Even in sleep it is possible to maintain the bond with the source of knowledge. Thus, even in the earthly aspect one may conform to a quality of the Higher World—continuity.

It is impossible to determine the structure of spatial forces; great numbers of intersecting currents fill Infinity, but not a single one of them will drop out of the web of the Mother of the World. The awakening of striving toward the higher worlds transforms all life. Not everyone can understand how the transformation of all life is taking place. One can repeat to oneself about continuity and weave each day a portion of the web.

150. People do not know how to find that which is most beautiful. They forget the best moments of enlightenment. But these hours are given to all, notwithstanding different conditions. A moment of enlightenment flashes out like a diamond. It is extremely brief, yet this brevity embraces a contact with the Supermundane World. Such touches are unforgettable! They are as torches on Earth and surpass the reason. One should preserve the supermundane sparks with solicitude.

151. Compulsion upon thought is a grave offense. It cannot be justified. It serves only to provoke new violations, and where then will there be an end to outrage? It is a mistake to presume that something created in the name of hatred can remain firm. Only construction, not subversion, can gather power for free thought.

Thought must be safeguarded. The very process of thinking must be loved.

152. The stratification of observations over the extent of many lives, laid in the depths of consciousness, is called dormant wisdom. It would be possible to carry out remarkable experiments by studying when man is drawing from his storehouse of knowledge. It is possible to make a comparison with atavism, which is manifested through several generations. Thus are displayed hereditary racial traits. But throughout his spiritual journeys man accumulates his own load, which he guards within his consciousness. It is instructive to observe the acquisitions of knowledge and inclinations already manifested in childhood, which cannot be explained in any other way except as former accumulations. The more so is it necessary to observe such individual propensities; they may indicate endowments which may later be damaged by an ugly upbringing. Dormant wisdom was already noted in deep antiquity, when questions of spiritual incarnation were sensibly understood. Intellectual advance resulted in a loss and impeded the development of the hidden forces of man.

153. People in whom the primary energy has ceased its movement have been called walking corpses. One can recall not a few people who continue to display the physical functions but whose energy has already become moribund. From such people one may receive the same impression as from corpses—for in essence they are indeed corpses. They no longer belong to Earth. They still move about and sleep and utter sounds. But the astral body, the husk, also moves and may be visible! Highly developed people can sense such corpses, forgotten on Earth. The faculty of such observation usually belongs to those who have been many times in the different worlds.

154. The world is making haste—here under the sign of war, there under a grimace of light-mindedness, here under a manifestation of hatred, there at the word of the head of the state. Each one is bent on his own acceleration, forgetting the fate of the overdriven

horse! Do not assume that it is possible to go on stratifying the energy endlessly when it is tensed.

155. Self-sacrifice is one of the true paths to Brotherhood. But why then is it enjoined, "Guard your strength?" There is no contradiction in this. The Golden Path, the combining path, affirms both qualities—achievement and caution. Otherwise all would be driven to suicide. Achievement is created in full consciousness and responsibility. Again someone may suspect a contradiction; but a higher devotion, an all-conquering love, can teach the combining of higher qualities. Madness does not bring achievement. Faint-heartedness cannot answer for true cautiousness. The conscious realization of duty prompts the right use of energy. Let people reflect about the concordance of qualities.

Madness and faint-heartedness are not suitable for the Path.

156. Much is said about the habitability of planets, yet rarely is there found one who senses such far-away conditions. The earthly nature of people does not take in such matters. Even the subtle existence does not embrace the idea of remote companions. Only the fiery consciousness, common to all worlds, can cognize and testify about distant lives. Consequently, it is possible only for the fiery essence to be concerned with such subjects.

Earth-dwellers who possess not only a developed subtle body but also a lofty fiery consciousness can have intimations about the far-off worlds.

157. Even under hypnosis people rarely speak about the Subtle World. An earthly will cannot force one to say anything about the Subtle World. What is the reason for this? It is to be found in Hierarchy, which guards against the useless spreading of information. There exists a popular supposition that in the Subtle World the individual principle predominates, whereas the higher the sphere the more is the principle of Hierarchy manifested. Dominating control by means of thought becomes feasible when the tight corporeal obstacles are discarded. Thus, when I speak about Hierarchy, I am only preparing you for the conscious acceptance of future advances.

There are two types of humanity: one can realize the entire constructive principle of Hierarchy, while the other contends in a most unrestrained manner against any approaches of Hierarchy. It can be noticed how much the Counsels of Hierarchy are rejected by this type of humanity. Such a degree of development, or rather of ignorance, can be changed only through tests in the Subtle World. Only there can spatial thought be sensed and the immutability of Hierarchic Infinity be felt.

One should not insist upon Hierarchy where it cannot be accepted. A man who is sufficiently experienced will respond at once to a word about Hierarchy. But the underdeveloped will not apprehend it.

158. Yet, for all that, information about the Subtle World does reach Earth. Such tidings are admitted as much as is possible without confusing the clouded consciousness. People should pay attention to children who remember not only former incarnations but also certain details of the Subtle World. Let these informations be fragmentary, yet for the observant scholar it all can be gathered into a whole necklace. The main thing is not to deny flatly that which seems extraordinary just at a given time.

159. Truly, the path of compulsion is like the path of narcosis. He who has been taking narcotics must increase the quantity of the poison taken. In the same way compulsion must be constantly increased, reaching the point of madness. Interruption of a compulsion carries the threat of domination by the dark forces. Therefore, compulsion is worthless for evolution. A conscious awareness contradicts compulsion. But lack of awareness is the ruin of the whole structure.

160. Be not surprised that the simplest examples often prove to be the most expressive. Setting forth on a distant journey, people look forward to seeing something attractive; if this does not happen, the journey turns out to be very abhorrent to them. Likewise, we should grow to love the idea of the Subtle World and the far-off worlds. One can so frighten oneself regarding the far-off worlds that even a move toward them will appear to be inadmissible. People usually have such a gloomy frame of mind toward everything of another world that they may be likened to a rueful traveler who has lost all his baggage. Let people be concerned with suggesting to themselves the best possibilities for success on the distant path. They will thus enter into the region of thought. It will be impossible for one to suffer who thinks beautifully! He will enter the Father's House, sensing in advance all the blessed treasures. Likewise must be comprehended the path to Brotherhood.

161. People like proofs by means of the most practical examples. Even though the inner meaning does not always coincide, evidence is always esteemed. The flow of a river is only slightly similar to the flow of life, yet this comparison long since has been applied. Likewise, an arrow does not fully correspond to a thought, yet the simile is customarily used in life. The consciousness of neophytes should not be too much burdened; let the load be such as they can carry on the path.

162. Ancient philosophy advised thinking about the far-off worlds as if taking part in the life on them. These indications have been given in various forms. Wherein lies their essential point? They cannot be an abstraction. The insistence in the indications about such participation shows that thought about the far-off worlds has great significance. The rays of the planets are powerful, and they exert influence upon humanity. But thought assimilates powerful currents, and in the thought process humanity can profitably accept the far-off worlds. Indeed, for such perception it is needful to think of them as about something close at hand. Thought creates around itself a particular atmosphere; in it the planetary currents can be transmuted to act beneficially. Whereas, the same currents, when met with a thought of negation, will yield grave consequences. It need not be considered that one must think incessantly about the far-off worlds. What is important is to direct to them a basic thought, and it will naturally flow along in a definite direction. Thought is of two kinds: the outward and the inward. The manifestation of outward thought can be recorded on an apparatus, but the inward thought is almost undiscernible, though it shows color and chemism.

Let thought about the far-off worlds be simple and without doubt; doubt is like a brown gas. Thus, we see that the ancient philosophy contains extremely useful indications.

163. Idiosyncrasies are inexplicable attractions or repulsions, and they appear as trustworthy evidences of reincarnation. No one can explain otherwise these irresistible feelings. It is vain to try to show them to be the effects of atavism, because it is possible to trace their independence of ancestral habits. The special force of such attractions shows that they are deeply implanted in a given individual. They are so firmly fixed in the consciousness that even hypnosis cannot overcome them. But if in individual cases the changes of lives were to be examined, then the attraction or repulsion would be found to be a natural effect of what has gone before. Thus, it is especially instructive to observe such inborn symptoms. They reveal both the capacities of the man and the kind of surroundings that are most favorable for him. Let us not forget that each plant needs its own soil; so, too, in the life of man, indispensable are the circumstances which are natural and peculiar to him.

Let those who rule learn how to arrange the human garden.

164. It is necessary to overcome the feeling of the void. Behind this illusion crawls much that is harmful; irresponsibility appears, and the maya of plunging into emptiness results, followed by dissolution in it. But then, what about the seeds that are indissoluble? From the realization of them will be built up an understanding of the space being completely filled. Such a condition will be the basis of responsibility. Thus, let us begin with the seed of spirit and then broaden the thought to include all space.

165. One should not be surprised that certain names are not pronounced. It is possible thus to understand the distinction between thought and word in the lower spheres. A thought is not perceived, and only the sound of a word can give away something held secret. Therefore, one should exercise discrimination in uttering names and in writing them, because writings may be seen.

166. Once again let us affirm the distinction between cooperation and Brotherhood. I note a puzzlement about this, as if the two concepts were identical. But they are different steps. Cooperation is definitely expressed in outward action, but Brotherhood is conceived in the depths of the consciousness. Co-workers may differ in the degree of consciousness attained, whereas brothers will sense each other precisely according to consciousness. Brothers may not be working together outwardly, but their thinking will be strongly knit together. They will be united freely; their unity will not be a burdensome yoke or a bondage. But precisely these brothers will understand unity as a powerful motive force for the good of the world. It is impossible to place limits upon such unity, for its basis will be love. Thus, cooperation will be a preparation for the realization of Brotherhood.

Often people are unable to perceive the boundary line where outward actions end and the invincible fundamentals begin. Do not think it superfluous to affirm the foundations of Brotherhood. It is hard to conceive what false imaginings arise during discussions about Brotherhood. Unprepared people think that Brotherhood is a legend, and that anyone can build spectral towers in his own way. They consider that unproven testimonies about Brotherhood cannot convince the reason; but no one is going to try to convince them. Likewise, no one compels collaboration. People themselves arrive at the necessity for cooperation. In the same way will they arrive at the reality of Brotherhood.

167. Rarely is found a ready consciousness, one which does not limit itself by fear, doubt, malice and hypocrisy. It can be seen that harmful limitation comes not only from without; first of all, it stirs about in the corners of the consciousness.

168. Rarely do people hear a cry for help and pass by without a heart tremor. Perhaps a brutalized heart will not lend a hand, but still it will be shaken. A cry for help may be expressed in words or in a single sound, but its heart-rending meaning will be the same. The cries of space likewise may be fragmentary and, according to the meaning of the words, insignificant, whereas their inner meaning is of importance. It need not be thought that the echo of distant thoughts has lost significance; even monosyllabic calls have effect. Sometimes a series of faces rushes past; they may not be familiar, still various frames of mind are felt. From such occurrences there may be built up a sensing of entire countries. One may understand where people are debating, where they are sorrowing, where they rejoice—such signals teach attentiveness. Not only complex reflections of events but also sometimes a solitary exclamation may give a feeling of the general moods. As on the strings the key of the entire musical composition is fixed by one chord, so in space each chord has a significance. On the field of battle a trumpet call decides the fate of an entire army. No one says that one should not harken to the distant signals. Many trumpets are sounding on Earth.

169. Is it possible to understand how much the mental sendings are being intercepted? It is difficult to imagine into what lateral canals energy can be directed. There may be accidental receivers, but evil entities may also draw near. Such interceptors may receive partial thoughts, and one may imagine the resulting frightful confusion of the networks. One should be armed for many eventualities.

170. The experienced guide shows the thirsty traveler the spring neither too soon nor too late. The guide knows how to prescribe repose according to the strength of the traveler.

171. One should receive guests graciously, but it is inadmissible to haul them in forcibly—every householder knows this. It is exactly the same in the application of psychic energy—one should not force it, but its manifestation should be received worthily. Let the ignorant prattle about the undesirability of applying psychic energy. When the energy is already at work it is impossible to deny it, and it remains to find its natural application. Let the learned tell what takes place if spatial electricity be limitlessly intensified. Let them tell how such excessive tension will end. It cannot be denied that at present spatial currents have been especially intensified. This is no time to deny them; it is needful to make haste with their application. Many times already has the danger of lower psychism been pointed out. Consequently, it is necessary to reflect about the higher energy, which is understood as spirituality.

172. Inexperienced physicians try to drive a disease inward in order even temporarily to evade dangerous symptoms—thus are established hotbeds of maladies. But the experienced physician tries to draw out the germ of the disease in order to eradicate it in good time. The same method ought to be applied in all sicknesses. It is better that a crisis be lived through than that a destructive collapse seize the whole organism. It is possible to live through a crisis, and such shock may call new forces into life. Whereas disintegration and rot but infect all the surroundings. Thus, let us understand it in forty ways.

173. Whoever defames that which is most exalted testifies to his own dissolution. The horrible denier reeks with corruption. He does not think about his unavoidable disintegration. People do not wish to notice what they prepare for themselves. Each murderer dreams about going unpunished. Where will he find this immunity?

174. Even during most tense days, think about construction. It is a mistake to strive tensely toward a narrowed goal; let construction proceed out of strivings toward the Most High. The shade of the valley should not hide the summits. One should not enclose oneself in an artificial circle. Of what use to one, then, would Infinity be?

175. Great Service has called forth everywhere much misunderstanding. To people it usually has the aspect of something unattainable. They hope that responsibility for such Service will pass them by. But let us reflect upon certain great Servitors. Let us see if They were unapproachable supermen. Pythagoras and Plato and Boehme and Paracelsus and Thomas Vaughan were men who bore their lamps amidst their fellowmen in life under a hail of nonunderstanding and abuse. Anyone could approach them, but only a few were able to discern the superearthly radiance behind the earthly face. It is possible to name great Servitors of East and West, North and South. It is possible to peruse their biographies; yet everywhere we feel that the superearthly radiance appears rarely in the course of centuries. One should learn from reality.

Let us not link ourselves with the vilifiers of Plato and the persecutors of Confucius. They were oppressed by citizens who were considered the pride of the country. Thus has the world raised its hand against the great Servitors. Be assured that the Brotherhood formed by Pythagoras appeared dangerous in the eyes of the city guard. Paracelsus was a target for mockery and malignance. Thomas Vaughan seemed to be an outcast, and few wished to meet with him. Thus was the reign of darkness manifested. Of course darkness, too, has its own laws. The dark ones watch intently a "dangerous" Great Service.

Let us apply examples of the past to all days of life.

176. One should understand that the forces of darkness are battling constantly against Brotherhood. Each reminder, even a small one, about Brotherhood will be violently assailed. Everything that can lead to Brotherhood will be condemned and defamed. Therefore, let us be on guard.

177. In the simplest examples there can be seen indications regarding forgotten fundamentals. The unaccountable whims of pregnant women will remind us about reincarnation, particularly when the character of the child is traced. Likewise, the latest medicine utilizes the concept of primary energy and points out the nervous origin of many ailments. Immunity is regarded as linked to a condition of the entire nervous system, thus putting forward the significance of the primary energy. How, then, may one not recognize it, when science is paying particular attention to it? Can one deny the basis of immunity? People are especially concerned about their health, yet at the same time they lose sight of the most precious factor. How, then, will thoughts about Brotherhood be created, if the fundamentals of life are left in neglect?

178. True, the quantity of insane people is monstrous. Not only must they be treated, but the cause of the increase in number must be discovered. The weak-minded also need surveillance. Madness is contagious. Weak-mindedness in childhood indicates subsequent abnormality through the entire life. People are agreed that the conditions of life are unhealthy; yet, in spite of this, every advice about improving conditions for health will meet with hostility. In this is contained the fear of any unsettling of the foundations.

It is appalling when that which is really most precious is in danger! Caution must be expressed in all of life. When I forewarn about the need of unity, I am anticipating the possibility of explosions. Amid fiery explosions one has to proceed as if on a tightrope.

179. Even for the earthly ear, it is necessary to listen in order to detect sounds. For the inner hearing more concentration is needed in order that the waves of space be heard. Let it not be thought that mental sendings can reach the destination without acceptance of them. Subtle sense also requires deep perceptions. To those who overconfidently assume that all beautiful birds come flying to them without expecting grain, let us say that each one must sow so that he may reap.

180. Let us refer, with regret, to the generally accepted idea of comfort and security. In it is contained torpor and vacuity. We learn to welcome all inceptions of thought, and We always esteem the pressure of a forward striving. A multitude of examples may be cited from physics and mechanics showing pressure as a motive force. For many, it is not easy to agree that pressure is but the gateway to progress. But if humanity will recognize this truth, in so doing it will also understand the meaning of progress. From the point of such cognition it is not far to Brotherhood.

181. A wayfarer cannot foresee all encounters, but he can find time to follow whoever is proceeding to the crossroads. He should not be distressed if by and by he may be left in solitude. There are paths difficult to traverse in company. Sustained attention to the goal leads to new traveling companions. On the path, it is necessary to keep to the goal with steadfastness.

182. The sword is tempered with fire and cold water; likewise, the spirit will be strengthened in the fire of exaltation and under the cold of defamations and ingratitude. One need not be surprised that vilification customarily attends each achievement. Service is attended by ingratitude. Such tempering has been observed since times immemorial, but the antithesis of fire and water is too little understood.

183. An artist once was ordered to draw a symbolic representation of faith. He executed a human figure expressing inexorableness. The face was uplifted to Heaven, and on it was an expression of unbreakable striving; the very look was filled with fiery radiance. The whole appearance was sublime, but from under the folds of the garment there seemed to be wriggling a small black snake. When the artist was asked what meaning was carried by this dark addition, which was out of keeping with the splendor of the picture, he said, "It is the little tail of unbelief."

The meaning is that even into a faith of strong degree there may often creep a small black tail of unbelief. Let it remind one of a venomous snake. Much poison is spread about by these little snakes. The most radiant faith becomes ineffective through a trickle of poison. Much has been said about the great power of faith, but it must be complete, unpoisoned faith.

184. Unbelief is the crystal of doubt. Therefore, one should distinguish the two. Doubt, as a form of unsteadiness, can be treated with psychic energy; but unbelief is almost incurable. The unbeliever plunges into an obscure abyss, to remain there shuddering until he receives a purifying shock.

It must not be thought that the path to Brotherhood is possible through unbelief.

185. You see how Our Word is defamed even by those who ought to be able to distinguish Truth. Therefore We point to the new ones, who are not infected with unbelief. Verily, unbelief is of many forms. It is concealed under diverse guises. It is needful to discern where the deadly little snakes are hidden.

186. People frequently hear voices that seem to be calling to them. Sometimes such calls are so strong that they force one to start and look around, though others present do not hear them. Can one possibly doubt that such spatial sendings do occur?

It is more difficult to understand why a sent thought which, by agreement, is to be received at a designated time is so rarely caught. First of all, people do not know how to put themselves into a definite frame of mind. Frequently, instead of receiving a thought, they thrust it away. Because of this, it is more often that thoughts arrive, which are not those agreed upon, but are ones which succeed in falling in with the rhythm of a mood. Still oftener can thoughts from the Subtle World be caught, because they may more easily harmonize with the energy of people. But people pay too little attention to thoughts from the Subtle World. One of the reasons is that the transmutation of language can be achieved only by strong, lofty spirits. On Earth, people often cannot understand the meaning of something that has been spoken, and it is even more difficult for them to adapt themselves to spatial sendings. Yet one need not be disappointed, for each attention to thought refines the consciousness.

187. The primary energy sometimes, like blood, needs an outlet. It is especially compressed during fiery tensions. Likewise, it is drawn to people who are in need of it. In this, it is necessary to distinguish those who are actually in need of it from vampires who devour it.

188. The Sacred Teaching cannot become congealed at one level. Truth is one, but each century, and even each decade, contacts it in its own way. New scrolls are unrolled and the human consciousness observes in a new way the manifestations of the

Universe. Even in its wanderings, science discovers new combinations. Upon such discoveries are the previously proclaimed fundamentals affirmed. Each transmission of the Great Wisdom is indisputable, but it will have its own followers. Those who honor Hierarchy reverence also its Messengers. The world lives by motion, and the issuance of the Sacred Teaching is evoked by advancing. The mediocre call such advancing a violation of foundations, but the thinkers know that life is in motion.

Even knowledge of languages increases the flow of new discoveries. How much more, then, will unfettered thought bring! Each decade reveals a new approach to the Sacred Teaching. The readers of a half-century ago read it completely differently. In comparison with those who are reading it at present, they emphasized entirely different thoughts. One should not speak about new Teachings, since Truth is one! New data, and new perception of them, will be only the continuance of cognition. Each one who impedes this cognition performs a transgression against humanity. The followers of the Sacred Teaching will not impede the path of learning. Sectarianism and fanaticism are out of place on the paths of knowledge. Whoever can impede cognition is no follower of Truth. The age of shiftings of peoples must especially safeguard each path of science. The age of the approach of great energies must openly encounter these luminous paths. The age of striving into the higher worlds must be worthy of such a task. Quarrel and strife is the lot of litterers.

189. It must be understood how inadmissible around the Sacred Teaching is evil talk. Disunity and dissolution is the lot of evil. On the step to Brotherhood, is evil talk appropriate?

190. The stupid are capable of affirming that Our

Brothers sow sedition and uprisings, whereas actually They are applying all efforts to conciliate the peoples. They are ready to carry on the heavy service of forewarning in time the persons upon whom the national destiny depends. They do not spare their forces in hastening to bring tidings. At the cost of disagreeable methods, They bear the Light, which the forces of darkness are trying to extinguish. Yet the sown seeds of good will not dry up, and in the ordained days the seeds will flourish. But what should those people be called who harm the good? They are capable not only of impeding Advice but of interpreting as failure the most natural consequences. By what measure will the stupid appraise effects? Why do they take it upon themselves to judge where success or failure has appeared? What could happen without the assistance of the Brotherhood? It is hard to imagine the evil interpretation that accompanies each Great Service!

191. To no purpose do physicians explain many ailments as purely physical manifestations. Catarrh, tuberculosis, colds in head and throat, and many other maladies are primarily of nervous origin. A man may feel a nervous exaltation and receive immunity, or through nervous shock may be left defenseless. This simple truth is not taken into consideration. Whereas the time is not far distant when the most diverse illnesses will be cured by means of nervous reactions. The treatment must be along the same paths by which consciousness is produced. It will be found that the most incurable diseases can be arrested by nervous reactions, and that without due concern about nervous forces the slightest indisposition may reach dangerous proportions.

192. The enemies of humanity not only have invented bullets which can pierce everything but they have in store new poisons. It is impossible to stop the flow of an evil will. Only selfless and constant reminders about good can bring the wave of pernicious influence to an end. Do not think that there was formerly less cruelty among people than at present; but nowadays it is justified by the most shameless hypocrisy.

193. Harmony is not always attainable, even if it is proclaimed verbally. It is a common error to think that harmony can be established by reason. Few realize that only the heart is the abode of harmony. People reiterate about unity, but their hearts are full of stinging arrows. People repeat many sayings from various ages about the power of unity, but they do not try to apply this truth to life. They reproach the whole world for dissensions and at the same time they themselves are sowing disunity. Verily, it is impossible to live without the heart. Heartlessness cannot find a harmonious abode. Not only do the sowers of disunity harm themselves but they also infect space; and who can foresee how far such poison may penetrate?

Do not think that enough has been said about unity and about creative harmony. On each page it is necessary to repeat about this very thing; in every letter unity and harmony should be mentioned. It must be kept in mind that every word about unity will be an antitoxin, destroying the spatial poison. Thus let us reflect about the good of unity.

194. Let us examine in what way Brotherhoods have moved around. Along these paths it is possible to learn about the movement of evolution. It should not be thought that Brotherhoods have hastily withdrawn into impregnable recesses. They have merely concentrated their forces in one strong place, both geologically and spiritually. It may be recalled that there have been hearths of Brotherhood in several countries, but at the approach of certain dates such hearths have been gathered together into one Stronghold.

195. It is useful to advise friends to send out mutually good thoughts at a definite time. In such an action there will be not only a strengthening of benevolence but also a disinfection of space, and the latter is extremely necessary. Poisonous emanations not only infect man but also are precipitated upon surrounding objects. Such sediments are eradicated with great difficulty. They can even accompany objects for long distances. In time people will distinguish the aura of such infected objects. Meanwhile sensitive individuals can feel the reaction of such stratifications upon themselves. Good thoughts will be the best purifier of one's surroundings. Affirmations of the sendings of good are still stronger than purifying incenses. But one should accustom oneself to such sendings. They need not be made up of definite words but only of a directed good feeling. Thus, in the midst of daily life it is possible to create much good. Each such sending is like a cleansing bolt of lightning.

196. Be careful with the throat center; as a synthesized central point it can definitely receive spatial influences. Since radio stations can exert an influence on the mucous membranes, many other reactions likewise can burden the centers.

197. Verily, the Teaching of Life is the touchstone. No one passes by without exposing his essential nature. Some rejoice, some are terrified, some are indignant. Thus, each one must reveal what is hidden in the depths of his consciousness. Be not amazed that the effect of the Teaching is so diverse and so striking. Narada similarly struck different sparks from human consciousnesses. If someone cannot contain the bases of justice and morality, let him display his own worthlessness. In short, let as few masks of hypocrisy as possible remain. Let savagery reveal itself, for it cannot long remain under a garment of deception. Likewise, let the youthful heart exult; it can manifest itself in joyful ascent. Thus, let the scale of the Teaching be also an indicator of the dividing line of humanity. Evil and good must be distinguished, but such discrimination is not easily made.

198. Among the external signs of fitness, pay attention to the wanderers. Something moves them and allows them no rest. More easily than others they realize the frailty of ownership. They are not afraid of distances; they are learning much. Among them may be messengers.

199. A man who has been saved may still imagine himself lost. One who is already perishing may think that he is victorious. All over the world crawls such lack of understanding. In reality, people are surrounded by phantoms. One can perceive the madness of whole nations. The Teaching can open many eyes and remind about the inviolability of the foundations.

200. He who appeals for better quality is already on the path.

201. The best curative products are often neglected. Milk and honey are considered nutritious products, yet they have been entirely forgotten as regulators of the nervous system. When used in their pure form, they contain the precious primary energy. Precisely this quality in them must be preserved. Whereas, the sterilization of milk and the special processing of honey deprive them of their most valuable property. There remains the nutritive importance, but their basic value disappears.

Indeed, it is indispensable that the products be used in their pure state. Thus, the animals and bees must be kept under healthful conditions, but all artificial purifications destroy their direct usefulness.

The ancient knowledge protected cows as sacred animals, and it wove an attractive legend about bees. But in time people lost the conscious regard for the remedies as first given to them. In the old manuals of healing, each remedy was looked upon from the standpoints of both usefulness and harmfulness. But such valuable substances as milk, honey, and musk carry no injury when they are pure. It is possible to point out many useful remedies in the plant world also, but the majority of them are best in the pure state, when the basic energy inherent in them, over and above so-called vitamins, has not been lost. The juice of carrots or radishes, or of strawberries, is best in the raw, pure state. Hence, it may be understood why the ancient Rishis subsisted on these wholesome products.

202. Resourcefulness and alacrity of thought can be developed by constant exercise. The first condition will be to think about these qualities; later it is useful to keep thought inwardly directed, so that it may remain alive during diverse occupations.

203. The seismograph indicates a continual trembling of the ground, but these earthquakes are by far not all that is noted by sensitive organisms. The reason for this is that Fire manifests in most diversified qualities. Moreover, the organism often registers insignificant signs that are confused with spatial influences. The human organism records a far greater variety of signs than is customarily thought. All that pertains especially to Fire is recorded by man. The explanations of this pre-eminence are quite scanty. People will talk about fatigue or indisposition, or about a certain frame of mind, but a reaction to the fiery element will not be mentioned. Actually, people do not picture to themselves that they are surrounded by Fire, which acts upon their primary energy. It would seem necessary to esteem everything which can strengthen the primary energy. It was said long ago that selfhood is extinguished by Fire. As long as they are not conscious of fiery baptism, people will think about themselves only; and as long as the most powerful element is not understood, the very concept of Brotherhood will be a barren skeleton.

204. Gradually it will become known that the legend is the true history; then documents will be found. Each revelation confirms the fact that truth lives on and must be perceived. Since myths live on, then too the history of the Brotherhood will acquire authenticity. It can be noted that information about the Brotherhood is especially suspected. Many circumstances are accepted quite easily, but the existence of the Brotherhood has a particularly striking effect. People are prepared to encounter an unknown hermit, but for some reason it is difficult for them to picture a society of such hermits. There exists an order of truths which meets with special opposition. It is not difficult to understand who is against the concept of Brotherhood. These creatures know perfectly well about the existence of the Brotherhood, and they tremble lest this knowledge reach the people. But all is accomplished in due time. If people do not know, still they are beginning to have premonitions.

205. Some messengers proceed with a mission, already knowing whence, whither and why—and how they will return. Others know but inwardly the Indication, and they complete the earthly path as ordinary citizens. Let us not weigh which of them accomplishes an achievement with the greater selflessness. Let people recognize that there exists a great number of degrees among the spiritual toilers. Chiefly there must be understood the result and the motive. It is not for us to judge which good deed is the higher. Each act is surrounded by many causes which the human eye cannot discern.

But let us value the good that is brought us and let us escort the messenger with friendliness. Precisely in this friendliness is found the key to success.

206. Likewise let us learn to distinguish the smallest signs. There are very many of them, flashing out as sparks; but let us not fall into bigotry or suspiciousness. The latter is to be distinguished from keenness. It has been said that keenness is straight, whereas suspiciousness is crooked. Besides, he who is suspicious is not pure and is not free. Knowledge must not be clouded by violence, neither external or internal. People often deplore cruelty, yet they are cruel to themselves. Such cruelty is worst of all. Apprehend justly the mean between apparent contradictions.

207. Take note by what unusual ways events are being molded. Actually, therein is contained the effect of new combinations of energies. During these days one should not make predictions according to old measures. Likewise, there may be unexpected indispositions. I affirm that the current of events is not to be turned aside by ordinary measures. Therefore let us be attentive.

208. People do not regard sensitiveness of the organism as an advantage. Even very enlightened people often are afraid of such refinements. In truth, a broadened consciousness is required in order to understand how indispensable for further advance is the acquisition of sensitiveness. Under the existing conditions of earthly life various pains may be expected, but certainly these sufferings occur, not as a result of sensitiveness, but by reason of abnormality of life. If there were an uninfected atmosphere, then sensitiveness would be seen as a true good; but people prefer to pollute the planet, if only they may dwell in the savage state. Do not think that words about savagery are an exaggeration. One may wear expensive clothing and still remain a savage. The more grave is the offense of those who have already heard about the condition of the planet and yet do not apply their efforts for the advancement of the Common Good.

209. Admonish people not to malign the Higher Forces. Madmen do not understand that their thoughts are refracted against powerful rays and smite the madmen themselves. If they do not fall dead at once, this still does not mean that their organisms have not started on the way to dissolution. One's own arrow finds the germination of an ulcer and brings it to the surface.

210. Dissolution of the organism is not spread over just one earthly life. One should not accuse one's parents; one should also discern one's own atavism. From absolutely healthy parents are often born very sickly children. The earthly mind will try to find the cause of it in remote forefathers, but he who knows the sequence of lives will reflect about causes contained in the person himself. In its lower and middle spheres the Subtle World preserves many bodily conditions.

It is of benefit to strive upwards.

211. Essentially, transition into the Subtle World ought to be painless. People having completed the earthly path ought to take up quite naturally the next proceeding. But they themselves complicate the solemn change of existence. They have propagated illnesses, and they pass them on to their near ones. They proceed to infect space, yet only by their own effort can they enter upon the path of purification. Compulsory prophylaxis cannot help fundamentally; a general conscious cooperation is needed. Compulsion can save only a small part out of hundreds of thousands of sick people. Rendering the planet healthful rests in the hands of all humanity. First of all, it must be understood that man makes healthy not only himself but also all his surroundings. In such a realization there will be contained true humaneness. Such a feeling cannot be commanded. It must come independently out of the depths of the heart.

Let the madmen not be surprised that We give so much attention to improvement of health. It is inadmissible to be an egoist and to think only about self. In both thoughts and actions we must spread abroad concern about better earthly conditions. Let us not hide ourselves in the folds of our mantles when it is necessary to exert all keenness and good will toward humanity.

212. Much is said about self-sacrifice and striving toward heaven, but there are examples of lofty self-sacrifice here on Earth. Every mother, under various conditions, in her own way expresses self-sacrifice. But let us be attentive, let us be able to discern the most well concealed signs of this great feeling, for it is so profound that it shuns expression. Among these beautiful blossoms there is to be found also the means for health improvement. Let us find best words, in order that man should not stumble. In this way also may the understanding of Brotherhood enter life.

213. From wherever good may come, let it not be rejected. The step of evolution must incorporate containment. And the good, too, must not be one combined with selfishness. Such a lower degree of good must be replaced by a higher. There is so much joy in

one's feeling when one can be exhilarated at the good of one's neighbor. But there is so much darkness in a personal appropriation of the General Good. Let the cruel ponder about what has been said.

214. I affirm that there are now many significant manifestations, but people are so blind that they do not see the prepared bread. People do not wish to recognize that which is already drawing near in full strength. Let travelers sing at the crossroads about the preordained Brotherhood.

215. Knowledge proceeds along the lines of both generalization and subdivision. Some scholars begin with the first steps of cognition to apply themselves to the former, while others cannot go beyond the limits of the latter. Sooner or later these too must turn to the method of generalization. One must learn to like this kind of thinking. In it is contained creativeness. Subdivision will be a preparatory path to the same goal. It is useful to be able to understand the distinction between the two paths. Indeed, there are at present many diligent scholars who are quite content with the second. But it is of little assistance when with each new cognition there is arising a synthesis of many branches of science. There is required great mobility of mind in order to be able to find comparison and confirmation from a most unforeseen domain of science. The ability to combine imperative evidences already demonstrates a lofty degree of consciousness. Much has been lost on account of needless subdivisions. There has even been noticed a sort of hostility between the separate branches of science. But are not the humanitarian and applied sciences branches of the same tree of Truth?

216. Let us not condemn the most painstaking investigation so long as it does not harbor calculated hostility toward a neighboring field of research. Let scholars find within themselves the resolution not to dismiss summarily anything which at the moment they do not understand.

217. People will say that rest is impossible in days of great confusion. Reply, "Let us not quibble about words." Rest, like Nirvana, is an effervescence which does not boil away. But if someone's strength is not adequate for such a concept let him be concerned with clarity of thought. Let him acknowledge that even in the hour of Armageddon it is needful to have a clear consciousness. If we lose clarity of thought in earthly battles, how can we maintain it during transition into the Subtle World? Each earthly impact is only a touchstone for our consciousness. Even during indignation one should not admit obscuration of thinking. Experienced people know that spatial currents are stronger than those of any human combat, yet during such powerful attacks one should clearly preserve the goal of existence.

Let those of little faith not bewail the fact that their rest is being disturbed. They change the significance of the best words and fall into vacuity. What could be worse!

218. During a thunderstorm it is advised not to run about nor make abrupt movements. Likewise, a harmonious condition is indicated during mundane storms. Let us not grasp at a cushion in order to hide from the thunder. Let us not rush to the smallest when we hear the knocking of something great. We must test ourselves in the most diverse circumstances; in this is contained the secret of diversification of incarnations. But people cannot understand in what manner a king is transformed into a cobbler.

219. Let us tell him who strives for practical occultism to reflect about incarnations, about the mystery of birth and of change of existence. It is inadmissible to by-pass manifestations of great significance. Such manifestations, before the eyes of all, can inspire thought about the essence of Be-ness. It is impossible to disregard such remarkable manifestations as the transmission and reception of thoughts. Not for derision are the recountings about little children who appear with remembrance of former lives and who can perceive the thoughts of others.

220. Each phase of the Teaching answers a particular need of humanity. The present time is distinguished by the shattering of morality. The help of the Teaching must be directed to the affirmation of moral foundations. The findings of science pursue a path different from the way of life; there results a particular kind of savagery, which is in possession of scientific instruments. A minority of highly enlightened workers stand out as rare islands in an ocean of ignorance. Literacy is by no means enlightenment; therefore, the advice is given to reinforce the heart as the focal point of enlightenment. Scientific and medical indications are given; they ought to help to restore the bodily and spiritual health. The more directly these counsels are accepted, the stronger will be their action. The embryo of enthusiasm grows into a beautiful inspiration. A drop of goodness is transformed into effective good. A grain of love grows into a beautiful garden. Who then would censure a desire to help a neighbor?

221. Each book of the Teaching carries an inner task. If brutality can make fun of Brotherhood, this will be the worst kind of savagery. Let people find the strength to restrain themselves from derision. Derision is not acuteness of mind. Humor is contained in a wise attitude toward events taking place, but the gaping mouth of the dull-witted is a disgrace to humanity.

Is it a game, when humanity becomes the plaything of madness? They will meet with success who uplift the Chalice with clean hands.

222. Unity is also needed there where the Teaching is being read. The reading alone is not a shield. There should be special joy at the assimilation of what has been read. In the course of the day each one can apply something from the Teaching; then comes the joy of unity.

223. The primary energy seeks admittance into all the nerves of humanity. It is, it does exist. It has been tensed by cosmic conditions. It is unfitting to ask whether one should develop it. It is impossible to develop the primary energy; one can only safeguard it against the waves of chaos. One should manifest great solicitude toward the treasure of evolution. Much was said in antiquity about the time when the primary energy would begin to be intensively manifested. People must not deny that which so imperatively claims its goal. Who is filled with such arrogance as to fall into denying the tidings of the epoch? Only the ignorant and those vaunting a false wisdom will begin fighting against the evidence. But let us not take to heart the attempts of the ignorant. They only make a wreath to each advice about helping humanity.

224. It is impossible to determine who may forcibly suppress searching observations. One should not cover the Light when it shines from the depths of cognition. Let the Light find the ordained paths. During a decline of morality, the attacks upon Light are unavoidable.

225. The domain of the most subtle energies is inexhaustible. It is possible to speak of learning about it but not of having the knowledge of it. I am speaking not for your disappointment but for your encouragement. If we make a cartogram of human penetrations into the frontiers of the distant energies, we find a very irregular line. People have hurled themselves into space, unsupported either by their fellow-men or by the Higher Forces; there has resulted the picture of a diver who has been let down at one point of the oceanic bottom and who has to give an elucidation of all underwater life. It is needful that all possible manifestations be observed and referred to laboratory investigations. So many times it has been said that a single investigator cannot succeed in observing all the threads of energies. Very often the spontaneous feeling of a child could prompt the necessary investigations. Not casually do I speak about physicians and schoolteachers; both have around themselves a broad field for observations. They can draw the attention of those around them to the loftiest subjects. They can be of much use to science, just as are meteorological stations. The most ordinary people can hear about various small manifestations, but who is to say where is the small and where the great? Often only one link is missing in that which constitutes a very important observation.

226. It is not easy to become accustomed to the thought that our sensations often depend upon spatial currents.

227. It is not easy to become accustomed to the fact that each minute the thoughts can bring a change of mood.

228. It is not easy to recognize that solitude does not exist.

229. It is not easy to feel oneself as belonging to two worlds.

230. It is not easy to realize that earthly life is a momentary vision. It is not easy to understand all this, though people ought to have premonitions of it right from birth.

231. Through the ages many erroneous interpretations have been made owing to the poverty of languages. People have turned to ciphers, to symbols and images, to inscriptions and to all sorts of hieroglyphics, but such expedients have only been of temporary help. Only the contemporaries could understand the meaning of such conventional accessories. In the course of ages they were obliterated, and new fallacies were built up. With difficulty does humanity retain informations for a single millennium. What, then, is to be said about periods of tens of thousands of years wherein languages themselves have been completely altered many times over! Isolated objects reaching down to our time cannot fully define the epochs which created them. Thus, it is needful to apply special circumspection to ancient epochs, which for us are only confused visions.

The time will come when clairvoyance, scientifically treated, will help to piece together the fragments of shattered vessels of ancient knowledge. Let the ability to decipher patiently the effaced signs be the distinction of a true scholar. He will apprehend too the meaning of containment.

232. Telepathy was recognized long before the transmission of thought. Sendings of feeling are more accessible to man than sendings of thought. It may be noticed that even the word telepathy is uttered far more complacently than thought - sending, which is frightening for many. Even in psychiatric hospitals a physician will readily agree about a telepathic manifestation, but as for the possibility of recognition of a definite thought transmission, this would denote a dangerous condition. Mesmerism was condemned but hypnotism is recognized. There is much injustice, and yet justice has to be restored.

233. In studying the psychology of prophets, there may be seen two phases of the manifestation. On the one hand, solitude may seem to be required, whereas on the other the prophet sometimes is illumined by a vision even when surrounded by crowds. The two conditions are not so contradictory as they appear. It is also possible to receive an impulse of energy from a crowd. There are no such conditions as could not prove to be conductors of the subtlest energies.

234. I continually speak about cautiousness, but I do not wish to inspire timidity in you. A cloud impels the gardener to take measures for protection, but he is not afraid of every whirlwind.

235. Hatred of humanity is reaching out for radical methods of destruction—by gases and poisoning. Let scientists make it clear that these gases do not disappear immediately but precipitate for a long time. Let the inventors of gases settle down in a house the walls of which have been rubbed with arsenic or corrosive sublimate, or other emanative poisons. By experience on themselves, on their eyes, skin and lungs, let them be convinced as to how long the emanating poisons continue to act. Moreover, in a large number of poisons their preparation works injury at great distances. Only criminal stupidity thinks that the damage will be done only to the enemy.

Likewise poisonous are the gases which irritate the mucous membranes. It cannot be permissible to poison a people, condemning it to maladies which make their appearance only after a passage of time. So-called enlightened rulers infect wide spaces and soothe themselves with the thought that the poisoning is harmless. Let them try living in a house which has been poisoned!

Among all the scientific discoveries gases and poisons will remain a disgraceful stain.

236. Some means must be found to enable people to understand the meaning of unity; otherwise, popular assemblies will resemble a bunch of balloons pulling to all sides. Some people assume that outward grinning alone should express unity. But the meaning of unified power remains alien to them.

237. Not only is one to be called a wayfarer who is already found upon the way but also one who has been making ready for the path. It is just the same with a world event: it has already been formulated, it already exists, even though the ship has not yet pulled up the anchor. It is needful to distinguish outer movement from inner readiness. Certain people attach no significance to inner readiness. For them, if something is not in motion before the eyes of everyone it means that it does not exist. Let us return again to medical examples. Many sicknesses may be in process inwardly, presenting no external symptoms. Only in the last stage are they manifested, when treatment is already useless. Let us not consider the process only when in its fatal stage. So it is too in human relations.

238. Many teachings enjoin abstinence from any killing. Indeed, what has been left unspoken is the question of the killing of the tiniest invisible creatures. Of course, what was considered was premeditated killing through evil will; otherwise with every breath man would be a murderer. The consciousness can whisper where the boundary line is. The heart can sense and can keep a man from killing.

If a bough has been senselessly broken let us nevertheless carry it to the temple, that is to say, let us be compassionate. The same feeling prompts one to guard against killing.

239. There is much fire. The far-off luminaries are aglow, and one can see them in the fire of the heart. Verily, there is much tension.

240. It may be noticed that sometimes especially large upheavals have far less destructive effect on the organism than small ones. The reason is that during the large upheavals psychic energy begins to act in a special manner, manifesting a powerful protection. During small agitations the protection may not be so strong. When I say, "Burden Me more when I go into the Beautiful Garden," this is not merely a poetic figure of speech but a practical indication. Long ago it was said that through great upheavals the spirit grows strong and the consciousness is purified. But in such processes the primary energy will be the principal factor. Therefore, let us not be distressed if it be brought into action in one particular way. It is far worse when something petty undermines the organism, and the salutary force is inactive. Such a situation must be recognized; otherwise people will begin to strive for the small and will be content with the mediocre. The store of psychic energy must be supplemented. Without pressure it does not receive the Higher Help. Even the enigmatic saying, "the worse, the better," has a certain foundation.

It is striking to observe how persecutions and oppressions multiply one's strength. One may marvel as to whence people draw the strength to endure and resist abuses. That same salutary energy which purifies the consciousness also creates an armor. Let us grow to love it, and let us not reject it light-mindedly. People say prayers for protection, yet themselves destroy the best gift.

241. In brotherhoods it is advised that mutual ridicule and defamation be avoided. Even in complex circumstances it is possible to find positive factors, and by such stones it is less dangerous to cross the stream. Abuse, like a thistle, grows rapidly, and with it there is no advance. Frequently, words are employed which call forth emanations not at all good. Each word impresses a glyph upon the aura. Man must take the responsibility for his own engenderments. Filth is unfitting in any brotherhood.

242. One should not draw arbitrary conclusions about the causes of the speeding up or slowing down of events. One must be able to take into consideration many conditions, of which the most important usually remain neglected. I instruct you to intensify your attention in order not to increase the complexity of the situation. People do not like to acknowledge, voluntarily or otherwise, how often a grain of dissension ruins the best combinations. Man can be likened to a magnet, yet even a magnet may become demagnetized if it be put in disadvantageous surroundings. Thus, one should accustom oneself to watching over the small grains. Unity cannot flourish if grit has been spilled on each wheel.

243. Cooperation is not easily achieved. For its assimilation a whole series of lives is sometimes required. People understand with difficulty the combining of individuality with communal labor. The human consciousness tosses like a ship in a storm, forgetting about synthesis.

244. "Friendship is in silence," an ancient Chinese once said. It can also be stated conversely. In such a higher state thought replaces many words. People can understand each other in different languages expressed mentally. The mystery of such thought transmission remains a great manifestation of the primary energy.

245. If people would deal with each other more trustingly, they could observe far greater manifestations of a cosmic nature. For example, if they were not so constrained about confiding their sensations, it would be possible to detect entire waves of transitory currents. There can be noticed particular throat sensations or heart pangs, or tension of knees and elbows. Currents can pass through all the centers. This will not be a sickness but a special indisposition. According to these symptoms it is possible to see where tension of currents is passing. But at least some confidence must be shown, without the fear of being laughed at.

246. The same fear impedes recognition of Hierarchy. In justice let us say that Hierarchy is far from any violence. It is ready to help and to send advice, but humanity is ready to suspect each good intention. Without trust there is no cooperation. Let us not forget that lack of trust is a sign of imperfection. A man filled with doubt will first of all not believe his neighbor. Let us not call these reminders moral counsels. Let them be called physical and mechanical laws. It makes absolutely no difference what the fundamentals of Existence are called, provided they be maintained and observed!

247. We never advise feigning a smile. As each unjust pronouncement is repellent, so, too, a hypocritical mask will be an indicator of falseness and of sickness of the aura. But we ask you to be more good in heart—this is the very best balm.

248. People are astonished at the quantity of crimes, but they forget about the incomparably larger number of evil deeds that are never detected. One may be horrified by the countless mental crimes which have not been legislated against, and yet they are destroying the lives of people and the life of the whole planet. One should reflect sometimes how much the fertility of the planet is diminishing, in spite of all the artificial measures taken at times by governments. It is possible to plant a grove of trees and, at the same time, poison and destroy entire forests. People marvel at the remains of primeval forest giants, but they do not ponder whether such giants can grow up nowadays. People strip away the virgin covering of the planet and then are astounded at the spread of sandy wastes. Upon recounting all the species on the planet one may be surprised at how little they are improved. Let us not consider certain peculiar cross-breedings that, like dropsy, can swell the size of certain vegetables. Such experiments have no influence on the general condition of the planet.

249. The heart keeps away many illnesses. It is wrong not to help the heart first of all. Perhaps the heart is outwardly calm yet needs to be given an impulse in order for it to have a strong influence on the other centers.

250. Is a deluge possible which can wash away entire regions? Can there be an earthquake which destroys whole countries? Can there be a whirlwind sweeping away cities? Can there be a fall of enormous meteors? All these are possible, and the swing of the pendulum can be increased. Does the quality of human thought have no significance? Thus let people reflect about the essence of things. It is very near to thought, and many thoughts are directed here from other worlds. Let us not blame sunspots alone.

A single thought about Brotherhood is already salutary.

251. Threat and violence are not of Our domain.

Compassion and warning will be the province of Brotherhood. One would have to be of a cruel nature to take a warning for a threat. People judge according to themselves; they try to insert their own meaning into each word they hear. It is instructive to give to a most diverse group of people the same simple text for interpretation. It is astonishing how differently the contents may be explained. Not only basic traits of character but also casual moods are reflected, causing the contents to be misconstrued. Thus, it may be confirmed that the evil see evil, whereas the good see good. The same truth carries through in all branches of knowledge. Only very keen eyes distinguish where is reality and where the mirage of a casual mood.

When man dreams about Brotherhood, let him first of all cleanse his eyes from the layer of accumulated dust.

252. Quite a few people think that Brotherhood does not exist at all. It may be that in the stillness of the night there sometimes flash out before them fragments of remembrances, but dullness of the reason obscures these dreams. True, in small recollections they may burn into the consciousness. Perhaps they cannot appear in a definite form, yet their meaning flashes like a flying arrow. A definite image may not arise for the reason that man has not been taught to think in images.

253. Likewise, man is not accustomed to distinguish coincidences from regular manifestations; he does not learn to follow the process of thinking, with all the attendant circumstances. So many disciplines are within reach of man in any condition whatsoever! With Us such natural accumulation is esteemed.

254. No one requires that a telephone call or a telegram be repeated twice before he will believe it. But it

works out otherwise in the matter of information from the Subtle World. For some reason people invariably insist upon repetition of manifestations, as if they could be convinced only through repetition; in such a manner much energy is wasted. Conditions have already become altered, but man wishes to turn backward. Much is made difficult by such retrogression.

255. Besides, people do not wish to observe how the process of thinking is dependent upon changes in surroundings. Such observations can identify many physical influences, and along with this they may reveal that along with visible influences others are continually to be perceived, invisible yet extremely powerful.

Whoever is ready for fraternal labor must know how to watch himself.

256. It may be noticed that people who remember their former lives belong to the most diverse levels. This merely illustrates that the other-world law is far more complex than people on Earth assume. All the more then ought it to be respected and studied. Such investigations must inevitably be of a fragmentary nature, yet this fragmentary information must constitute a convincing chain of facts. The quicker such an earthly chronicle can be begun, the sooner will the truth be revealed. It must be understood that it is not Our custom to demand blind faith. What would be the use of such a demand, since observation and attentiveness yield better results?

It has been said that the web of the Most High consists of sparks; consequently, if one discerns even a single spark it will already be a big attainment. But in such experiments it is possible to achieve success only through mutual trust. Valuable information can be brought even by children, country folk, and various workers in whom even a single spark with which they have come in contact has caught hold. Very often people actually preserve some memories but are ashamed to talk about them. Such hiding places must be approached solicitously. They will not be revealed to an arrogant interrogator or to a hurrying passer-by. Moreover, earthly law prohibits touching upon what is professed to be sacred. Physicians frequently call such confessions madness.

We have already said that all questions concerning the inner consciousness must be severely tested, and if, out of a hundred dubious and obscure communications, one will prove to be authentic, this will already be a success. Thus, let us seek Truth.

257. Let quests of Truth be not full of gall. A man who has lost some object in his home is immediately irritated. What, then, will happen in world-wide quests?

Verily, a kind cooperation is indispensable.

258. Seeds may be scattered by the whirlwind; they may be nibbled by birds; they may be washed away by a downpour of rain—many are the causes and the effects. It is especially difficult for man that he cannot predetermine the result of a sowing. But because of this he should not distribute arbitrarily the results of labor. Man must clearly picture the goal of his work, but the paths of movement and the new obstructions must not distress the worker. In the earthly way it is not easy to reconcile oneself to the thought that seeds can sprout in unexpected places. But let man not forget that the vitality of a seed is great. Thus let us sow, without thinking where the beautiful garden will spring up and expand. A man may select for his garden a splendid place, according to his way of thinking, while the place next to it may prove to be a far more fertile soil where even a seed brought by the wind will flourish. Thus let us sow, having no doubts about the vitality of seeds.

The basis of Brotherhood is trust in work.

259. Sometimes it may seem that an instruction has not been given clearly enough, but is this really true? Will not some of our transitory moods be false interpreters? In time the mood will disappear and the true features will appear. It will then be possible to recognize that the instructions were unalterable. Thus is forged the approach to Brotherhood.

260. Let us not be astonished that after an indicated date the tension, as it were, increases. Let us not forget that this is an effect of what has gone before. But the sowing of causes may already be diminished.

261. Putting on the earthly envelope man has to create good, thus perfecting himself—so speaks wisdom from times immemorial. And over the Gates of Brotherhood constantly shines this Principle. It will not be contradictory to those who understand the unmanifested, endless evil of imperfection. Though imperfection be inevitable, nevertheless there do exist branches of labor which embody good in its full significance. Is not the work of the husbandman good? Is not beautiful creativity good? Is not craftsmanship of lofty quality good? Is not knowledge good? Is not service for humanity good? It can be affirmed that the essence of life is good, yet man in his unwillingness for perfectment prefers to remain in ignorance, that is to say, in evil.

262. Fire is required for tempering the best blades. Without fire the centers of the organism cannot be refined. Inflammation of the centers is unavoidable, but one needs only to be very careful during such periods. A red-hot blade is easily broken; likewise is a glowing nerve filament easily torn. Therefore, let us be very cautious. Such circumspection indicates knowledge of the situation.

263. Picture a house filled with people who know about some important event, but among whom is one who does not know what all the others are thinking about. There will be a great difference between those who know and the one who does not know. Even judging by externals, one can form an opinion about the obvious difference. He who does not know will begin to feel troubled, to glance about, and to listen; he will be suspicious and look around in a hostile way. The more irritation he may feel, the further he will be from a solution of the enigma. In such simple examples there can be observed the effects of thought and the causes which impede their perception. For the grasping of a thought, first of all, irritation is not useful. There may be excitement or tranquillity, but absolutely no anger or irritation.

Let those who propose to observe thought transmission keep in mind that there may be obstacles which appear insurmountable, but which are easily set aside by man himself. The quieting of irritation only seems difficult. Let us not forget to gaze at a column which represents space, and try to imagine where irritation could be marked on it—no place will be found for it, and it is the same with egoism in the face of Infinity.

264. Comparison of the smallest with the greatest enables the finding of equilibrium. On each difficult path even a smooth rock will furnish some foothold. But the smooth surface results from a great number of streams. Thus, let the wayfarer not think that it is difficult for him alone.

265. An ancient adage says, "He who thinks about death summons it." Likewise, physicians also have sometimes noticed that thought about the end brings it near. Much of folk wisdom contains a particle of truth. But one must first of all reflect—is it possible to be occupied with thought about that which does not exist? It is time for people to recognize that life is uninterrupted. Thus the attitude toward earthly existence will be completely altered. For proper evolution it is necessary to speedily affirm the right point of view toward a continuous life. Science must come to the help of dispersing gloomy fallacies. It is not for man to think about the grave, but about wings and ordained beauty. The more clearly man instills in his consciousness the beauty of the worlds, the more easily will he be receptive to new conditions.

266. The Teaching of Life must first of all affirm the concept of life beyond the limits of the earthly envelope. Otherwise, why the concept of Brotherhood if that which is most precious must be developed for only a few decades? Not for tomorrow must consciousness be amassed, but for eternal paths into Infinity. It is useful to repeat this truth in the light of day and at night.

267. Cooperation can have beginning and end, but Brotherhood, once established, is inviolable. Therefore, let us not be light-minded toward this concept fixed in the foundation. During all existences Brothers will meet together and affirm labor in common. One should rejoice at such a possibility, which will not be exhausted throughout the ages.

268. When people begin to distinguish causes from effects, much is perceived, but up to the present people recognize only effects, and this only in the crudest degree. No one wishes to understand that a certain time must elapse between cause and effect. When a subtle consciousness discerns causes, it is usually subjected to ridicule. A gross eye does not see what has taken place, and the ignorant proclaim that nothing has happened. Therefore it is time to direct thought to the root of the matter. However this is not easy, for confidence has been stifled, and thus the energy of perception has been brought into inaction. Many cases could be cited when cognition was able to foresee in causes the beginning of effects, but a little unbelief washes away all possibilities.

269. Chaos is jealous and raging. It overwhelms wherever the least vacillation is found. Chaos loses no opportunity of breaking through a weak barrier. It may be noticed that treacheries take place on the eve of especially useful actions. There has not been a case when treacheries were perpetrated aside from particular dates when paths of progress had been already molded. Actually, darkness and chaos cannot endure anything constructive. They watch over pathways and seek whoever is capable of helping them. Many examples can be named, but on the other hand there are many indicative actions when heart unity has overcome darkness. Therefore, it is so needful to guard the concept of Brotherhood.

270. Sacred pains do not pertain to any form of disease. Such an unusual condition can surpass all known illnesses. Everything becomes so tensed that the least shock can break the tautened strings. As has already been said, such a condition is aggravated still more by the unnatural condition of the planet. The sickness of the planet threatens the heart with pressure. In olden times sensitive organisms were guarded for a profound reason. The term sacred pains ought to direct attention to the heart that has contacted the finest energies. Such hearts need to be guarded, they are as conduits of the higher tension. They need to be guarded both in the home and throughout life. If physicians were less self-opinionated they would strive to observe such rare manifestations. But unfortunately, all peculiar symptoms rather repel indolent observers. Whereas side by side with the mechanization of life the study of higher energies must go on.

271. Sometimes there result converse effects when people approach the higher energies with crude methods. For example, let us take eyeglasses devised for observation of auras. The principle is not bad, but the means are crude and affect the eyesight adversely. Whereas the refinement of senses must not impair the natural state of the organism. Thus, the use of radium has proved destructive, whereas radioactivity as a principle is curative. Likewise, alcohol becomes a destructive narcotic instead of a medicinal remedy. The examples are many. The principal cause lies in unwillingness to realize the bond of the organism with subtle energies.

Brotherhood and cooperation should assist the refinement of thinking. Refinement of thought provides a passageway to refinement of life. Refinement is also upliftment and growth.

272. There is nothing astonishing in the fact that even an absolutely simple man can see radiations—the causes for this are many. He may be an unusual man by reason of his former lives, or there could be expressed in him this special quality among others less pronounced. Such isolated cases are not rare. It may be noted that even unlettered people may possess extraordinary perceptions. They do not know why such knowledge comes to them, since they are without any guile. Such qualities, though obviously expressed, have nothing in common with the accumulations from past lives. So many chemical reactions can arouse individual qualities, which spring up and then can temporarily disappear. Only an understanding of altered spatial currents can explain the changes taking place in the organism. You know that sight and hearing and all one's sensations vary under the influence of currents. One may be assured that such fluctuations take place not only on manifested dates but also aside from human reasoning. Actually, only external conditions can create such inexplicable manifestations.

273. A wise philosopher, having been sold into slavery, exclaimed, "Thanks! Evidently I can pay back some old debts." An emperor, nicknamed the Golden, was terrified, "Luxury pursues me. When will I be able to pay off my debts?" Thus have wise people thought about the quickest payment of their debts. They understood that former lives surely do not elapse without incurring indebtedness. But a man with much income must make haste in settling his accounts.

274. If someone assures you that he is neither for nor against something, regard him as being against it. Among these voiceless ones there are far more opponents than among the shouters. People hope to conceal their opposition under a mask of hypocrisy. Therefore it is especially valuable when a man has the courage to speak his opinion. However, for correctness of appraisal it is needful to realize Brotherhood as the lever of the world. One should not recognize only one's own personality, because isolation does not exist, and he who tears himself away falls into the lower strata and injures himself.

275. It is correct that people should have identical control over paired organs, but such control can only begin in childhood. A child has equal use of his hands, but in examples surrounding him he sees a preference for the right hand. In schools it is already too late to restore equality. Only amid the first flashes of consciousness can a child avoid the prejudices of adults. Too little attention is paid to the curiosity of children. One can learn much from how quickly they notice their surroundings.

276. The Teaching can be assimilated by children extraordinarily quickly, provided the child's peculiarities be observed. In a great degree he remembers what has been absorbed earlier, and it is especially useful if instead of new knowledge the child be helped to recall what has already been implanted in him. In this way it is easier to absorb new subjects later, but one must be observant.

277. Each true worker sometimes experiences, as it were, the fall of all his work into an abyss, moreover an abyss which is unfathomable. Thus the spirit of the worker suffers a most dangerous predetermination. A weak one senses the abyss and falls into despondency, but a strong one recognizes the touch of Infinity. Many observations and experiments confront a man before he can encounter joyfully the face of Infinity. Gone will be regret for human creations which have been dissolved. They, even the most sublime ones, will be dispersed in Infinity. The earthly mind does not realize where its accumulated treasures can be made manifest. A man wishes to bring good to humanity, but instead of the fruits of his labor there lies before him an unfathomable abyss. A formidable mind may shudder at that, but the tempered, manifested warrior of labor sees before him, not a chasm but the radiance of Infinity.

Brotherhood is needed in all its mutual assistance. Who, then, if not a Brother, shows the Light of indestructible toil? In space grows each sprig of labor. That which is created does not disintegrate, but sows around itself divisible, innumerable forms. True blessing is in the ever-presence of Infinity. It is possible to populate it with beautiful forms.

278. It was said in antiquity, "All people are angels." Verily, people are the messengers of the far-off worlds. Hence great is their responsibility. They rarely take the responsibility of carrying that which is entrusted to them and are not even distressed at losing the treasure. Only a few individuals may sorrow that they have forgotten something they have heard. Let people not forget that they are messengers and a bond with the distant worlds. Such a consciousness in itself beautifies everyday life.

279. It is already known that human saliva may be either curative or poisonous. But in this circumstance a very important condition has been forgotten—namely, that the poisonousness of saliva does not depend upon disease. Likewise its curative quality remains during certain illnesses. This means that such properties are not only physical but they manifest subtle substances which are connected with psychic forces. The transmutation of psychic energy into an actual material substance will be in itself an affirmation of subtle energies. One should observe such manifestations in animals and even in plants.

The dates are already approaching when the cooperation of material and psychic forces must be formulated, otherwise humanity will begin to poison itself with unrealized energies. Not so dangerous are the increasing numbers of humanity as is its poisoned condition.

280. Disciples noticed that the Teacher often retired to the bank of a stream and gazed intently at the running waves. They asked, "Do the waves actually help pranayama?" The Teacher replied, "You have

guessed rightly, because the rhythm of waves is a marvelous alternation which occurs only in nature. In this multiformity there is an amazing unity." Thus, pay attention to all movements occurring in nature.

281. In an attempt to be wily people frequently say that many conditions prevent them from creating good. Whereas in each and every condition man can create good. This is the privilege of the human state.

282. In the Brotherhood each one works as much as he can. Each one helps in accordance with the measure of his forces; each one does not condemn in his heart; each one affirms knowledge according to his experience; each one lets no time escape, for it is irrecoverable; each one is ready to lend his strength to a Brother; each one displays his best quality; each one rejoices at the success of a Brother. Are these principles too difficult? Are they supernatural? Are they beyond human strength? Do they require super-knowledge? Is it possible that only heroes can understand unity? Precisely for the sake of comprehension examples have been given of the better people becoming physicians, cobblers, weavers, butchers, in order to infix better thinking through different kinds of labor.

Over and above man's work stands the manifestation of woman. She leads, she inspires, she guides on all paths, and she displays an example of synthesis. It is astonishing how quickly she enters any domain. From Earth up to the far-off worlds she succeeds in weaving wings of Light. She knows how to preserve the Chalice in different atmospheres. When We speak about cooperation, We always point to the achievement of woman. The domain of Brotherhood is the field of cooperation.

283. Whoever in speaking attributes the Teaching of Life to himself falls into falsehood. The Sources of the Teaching are beyond human limits. The Truth has been written down in Infinity, but each day it reveals a new hieroglyph of its eternalness. Mad is he who while on earth arrogates to himself the Teaching of Life. The loftiest sage considers himself a messenger. Not the new is proclaimed, but what is needed for the hour. The steward summons to the meal; this is not new, but for the hungry it is extremely important. So much the worse if someone obstructs the call to a meal. He who hinders forges shackles for himself.

284. If someone turns away a hungry man, he is near to being a murderer. Seldom is there not a bit of bread in the house. Hardness, avarice, cruelty, are not on the threshold of Brotherhood.

285. Dispassionateness is not heartlessness or indifference. When people read historical chronicles, they are not irritated, because these writings belong to the distant past; and the experience of life teaches that almost all received communications also refer to the past. Likewise, experience whispers that the future can direct thoughts above and beyond irritation and disturbance. Thus, only the future is liberated from passion. From it is born active dispassionateness. Usually people upbraid one for this concept, confusing it with selfhood; but it is better to attribute it to justice. Only the future, not littered by the confusion of the recent past, can enable one to think rationally. Thus let us carefully analyze the significance of many concepts that have been undeservedly abased or exalted.

286. Verily, human speech should be guarded against various disfigurements that are ugly and unexpressive. Furthermore, language needs to be cleansed of certain archaisms based on long outmoded usages. People often utter words without taking into consideration their significance. Thus they fill their speech with meaningless names and concepts. Indeed they would have to laugh if they were to reflect upon the real meaning of what they had said. So, too, in everything one should abandon the outlived, which has lost its primary meaning.

287. Let us be together; let us stand steadfastly for the future. Only by taking such a devoted stand will we be as if in an impenetrable armor.

288. In many industries workers inhale and touch many chemical substances. At first glance it appears that such contacts pass without injury, but this will be only a superficial judgment. It can be proven that different branches of work give rise in time to identical illnesses. The first intake of a dangerous substance is not noticeable in its influence, but by constant repetition it takes possession of the entire organism and renders it incurable. I am speaking about this because of another effect, about which people still think too little. They have already noticed the moon's influence; even physicians have paid attention to the influence of the moon upon many human states. But such influences take place repeatedly. The effects may not be noticed with the human eye, but the rays of the luminary dominate not only the physical side but also all feelings. In this it can be noticed that people with strong psychic energy are less subject to the influence of the rays upon their psyche. Thus, the natural development of psychic energy will be an excellent prophylaxis. It will also be so in relation to many other currents; therefore neglect of psychic energy is ignorance.

289. If a messenger sets out upon the path with a definite mission and then forgets it, what should he do? Should he hope that his memory will be cleared up while on the way, or should he hasten to inquire of the one who sent him? Knowing how to inquire will already be an attainment.

290. If the psychic energy of even one individual is a prophylaxis for physical health, then how much more powerful will be the influence of unified energy. The meaning of Brotherhood is contained in the unification of the primary energy. Only broadening of consciousness helps to realize the significance of harmony of energy. On all the planes of life it manifests its beneficent force. No doubt you have been asked many times how to develop psychic energy and how to realize its usefulness. But it has been said enough that the heart that aspires to higher quality of all life will be the conductor of psychic energy. No forcible, conventionally accelerated movement toward a display of the heart's action will be useful. The heart is a most independent organ; it may be set free toward good, and it will hasten to be filled with energy. Likewise, only in friendly communion is it possible to secure the fruits of unified energy. However, for this it is indispensable to understand what harmonious agreement is.

291. It is especially difficult to perceive the instantaneousness of action of the subtle body. People have so bound themselves with the conventional concept of time in its earthly sense that it is impossible for them to get away from the idea of lengthiness of time. Only those who have already become accustomed to issuing forth into the Subtle World know how much one can feel in an instant. Much can be sensed in the spirit, and each perception must be preserved.

292. Treatment by means of music is already being applied, but the effects are not always perceptible. The reason is that it is not customary to develop perception of music. From childhood one should be accustomed to assimilating the beauty of sound. Musical faculties are in need of education. It is true that in each man has been implanted an inclination for sound, but without cultivation it remains asleep. Man ought to hear beautiful music and song. Sometimes a single harmony will awaken forever a sense of the beautiful. Yet great is ignorance when the best panaceas are forgotten in the family. Especially, when the world is quaking from hatred, it is indispensable to make haste in opening the ears of the young generation. Without realization of the significance of music it is also impossible to understand the sounding of nature; and, of course, it is impossible to think about the music of the spheres—only noise will be accessible to the spirit of the ignorant. The song of waterfall or river or ocean will be only a roar; the wind will not bring melody and will not resound in the trees as a solemn hymn. The best harmonies vanish for the unopened ear. Can people accomplish their ascent without song? Can Brotherhood stand without song?

293. Similarly, for treatment with color the eyes must be opened. Often a single contact is enough for the eyes to perceive forever the beauty of color, still an enlightened touch is needed. Even if the eyes have already been opened through former accumulations, it is still needful that the call to "Look!" should resound.

And in Brotherhood, first of all, the members hearten and inspire each other with affirmations of beauty.

294. One should make rational use of external energies. It is criminal to subject human organisms to the reaction of insufficiently investigated energies. Thus, it is easily possible to condemn multitudes to degeneration. Such degeneration takes place imperceptibly, nevertheless its effects are horrible. Man loses his best accumulations, and there results, as it were, a paralysis of brain similar to opium poisoning. The appearance of opium smokers sometimes resembles poisoning by charcoal fumes or benzine. Humanity should be urged to take measures so that cities be not poisoned by benzine and petroleum. The danger of insanity is growing.

295. Solemnity should be strengthened by the concept of Brotherhood. It ought not to remain an empty sound. To affirm solemnity means to sing hymns to the rising sun. It must be realized what purification is vouchsafed at being filled with health-giving solemnity. All the proposed concepts have a significance both elevating and curative. We suggest all that which can also fortify the body. Let us not think that exalted concepts are manifested only as exaltation; they also constitute salutary means that strengthen the organism. One should realize the power of beneficent concepts.

296. Solemnity should be proclaimed when Infinity is realized. Some are surprised at the fact that the book *Infinity* was given before succeeding books. But how would it be possible to understand *Heart*, *Hierarchy*, *Fiery World*, and *Aum* if the concept of Infinity were not sent in advance? All the aforementioned concepts cannot be in a finite state. Man cannot assimilate any of them, if he does not breathe in the call of Infinity. Can the human heart be considered as a lower material organ? Can Hierarchy be located in a limited space? The Fiery World begins to shine only when its flames flash out in Infinity. If Aum is a symbol of the higher energies, can they possibly be limited? Thus, let us pronounce Infinity with solemnity.

297. After the grandeur of Infinity is it possible to speak about simple earthly unity? Even if this is not asked, still many will think thus. But who, then, has said that earthly unity is something simple? In order to understand it realization of synthesis is needed first of all. But such generalization can come about only through realization of Infinity. Earthly unity is certainly not simple!

This word is uttered often, but rarely is it applied to action. Can many people get together in unity? No sooner does the principle of labor bring them together, than occasions for discord arise. It is impossible to explain what unity is if in the heart there is no conception of Great Service.

298. Only the call to Brotherhood can sometimes flash out as lightning. Let people think that Brotherhood is inopportune, that it is unattainable; but for all that even a savage heart will begin to tremble, even a hardened, embittered heart will not pass by such a reminder of something forgotten. It is necessary to find the simplest words, for people are expecting the simplest. People can accept a good word if persuaded that it will make better their way of life.

299. You are becoming convinced that people are open to cognition. Such a step of evolution is not accidental. Many shocks and much trepidation have compelled hearts to shudder and begin to resound. Verily, heavy must be the burden in order to enter the Beautiful Garden.

300. If the planet were to arbitrarily slow down or accelerate its motion, one can easily imagine all the ruinous consequences. Hence it is so important to assimilate the significance of rhythm. Speaking of human labor, one should continually insist upon rhythm. Constant and rhythmic work produces the best results. The labor of the Brotherhood serves as an example of this. Rhythm is indispensable because it also affirms quality of work. He who is conscious of rhythm loves his work. But the magnet of love is not easily intensified. Without it reprobation and repulsion arise. Without it loss of quality and waste of time and materials result. It is needful to speak more often about the rhythm of labor, otherwise even gifted and capable workers will lose their aspiration.

The production of worthless objects is an offense against the people. In striving to Infinity it is needful also to think about the quality of all labor. Each Teaching is first of all concerned about quality, and thus each task must become a lofty one.

301. In view of the expanding growth of the domains of labor, quality has become especially essential. Cooperation of different fields requires an identical lofty quality—this refers both to mental and to physical work. In the province of mental labor a divergence of strivings is noticeable. Opinions may be diverse, but their quality ought not to be ugly. There can be great knowledge and small knowledge, but both can fraternally follow along in perceptive striving. This will not be murdering knowledge. Indeed, such killing is equivalent to taking away life. So many embryos of attainments can be strangled by killers of knowledge.

Not only is knowledge precious, but equally valuable is the process of acquiring knowledge. At one time philosophers compared such a process to a higher enjoyment. The more deeply it can be felt, the greater the joy. But if in the accumulation of knowledge there enters the bondage of egoism, then not joy but rancor boils up. Conflict is inseparable from the accumulation of knowledge, but it also should be a treasure trove. None of the paths of knowledge will be misanthropic.

302. Again let us delve into the concept of mood. During transmission at a distance there is frequently noticed some impeding circumstance, which colors the thoughts and gives them another meaning. The human frame of mind tints all of life in unexpected colors. Our moods are called tacit thoughts. They are not put into words, but they have an influence upon mental energy. It can be easily shown that both the sender and the receiver are in opposing moods, consequently the transmission of thoughts is not precise. From this it should not be concluded that thought transmission cannot be accomplished; for it can be truly precise when concomitant conditions have been provided against. Mood will be the most manifest of such conditions, but its regulation is entirely possible. Organisms fraternally attuned will resound without superimposed stratifications.

303. Certain disciples of lower degrees are afraid to rise on the ladder of ascent, wishing to avoid the responsibility which grows with each step. Such light-minded disciples even suppose that their sojourn on the lower steps is more interesting. They are content with the physical manifestations of materialization and with similar irresponsible occupations. Nevertheless, they know that eventually each disciple must manifest himself in daily labor and undergo the attack of chaos. This is not so agreeable for the light-minded. Thus, Brotherhood itself appears difficult to them.

304. People hope that that which is most difficult will pass, but beyond it will begin blissful Amrita. What will they think if they are told that after the difficult comes the still more difficult? Perhaps people will attempt to leap away from the human path? But whither can they depart? Only he who is not terrified by the most difficult will feel the bliss of Amrita.

305. Let us look at the apostates, who appear in all ages. It is possible to notice many common traits in their betrayals. Likewise it is possible to notice how, according to karmic paths, they have found the way to persons whose manifestation has been hateful to darkness. There can be discerned the same modes of falsehood that they have made use of in different languages. Moreover, it can be affirmed that not a single betrayal has succeeded in darkening the name of the one persecuted—so says the truth of all ages.

One may find unusual writings about unprecedented attempts of darkness to subvert the inceptions of knowledge.

306. There are different kinds of expectation: there is revealing expectancy, and there is also obstructive expectancy. In the first the heart awaits, but in the second the I—self—awaits. A thought, even the loftiest, flies with difficulty through a wall of egoism. It droops at the sharpened stakes of egoism. Jagged is egoism, broken up with envy and savage malice. Such an encounter cannot admit a beautiful thought. Much takes place perceptibly in the process of receiving a thought. There occurs an instant of calm before the arrival of the higher Messenger. But can puffed-up egoism sense this most blissful moment? The heart alone knows how to be filled with expectation. Only the heart does not cry out, I am waiting! Very much egoism sounds in such an I. But to await with the heart, this means to already have a premonition. There is much joy in such a feeling. The ancients called it the guide. I affirm that a premonition is already the opening of the gates. The heart is a cordial hostess; it foresees how to meet the guest from afar. It is needful to exert one's best feelings in encountering thought.

307. It is said that thought must be met in silence; such a condition is useful but it still does not express all the subtlety of the sensation. Actually, solemnity will be the best definition. But for solemnity purity of heart is needed.

308. A physician can feel solemnity; even the sight of disease does not darken the heart that is aglow with help for a fellow-man. It is amazing to observe how good becomes curative. Compassion has its roots in the heart alone. Thus are brotherly qualities accumulated.

309. Under the influence of thought it is possible not to hear even nearby music—thus is demonstrated the power of thought over the physical organism. Likewise, amid the waves of life it is possible not to notice the touch of a Brother's hand, but it can still bring equilibrium. And similarly, music, though not heard, contributes to the exaltation of thought. With Us the unfelt touch of a Brother is called by a secret word. It is not to be expressed by verbal signs, but is reflected upon the heart; therefore the heart is called the reflector of Brotherhood.

310. Do not consider absurd the testimony of the three aviators who saw horses at a great altitude. Such a vision is possible for several reasons. Motion itself can call forth forms connected with it; then, too, speed can concur with manifestations from the Subtle World. As before, it is needful to advise noticing such signs. One should not inevitably consider them as omens, but one should accept them as facts from the spheres of the Subtle World. There are not a few such manifestations, but extremes of attitude toward them are not permissible. People refer to them either with contempt or with absurd exaggeration; rational observation is rarely encountered.

311. A special science shows how to find a rational attitude toward different subjects. Such an attitude engenders a true understanding of Brotherhood. Preservation of sacred concepts indicates development of consciousness.

312. Swiftness of motion up to a certain extent furthers intercourse with the Subtle World. A vortex of movement, as it were, sweeps away the dusty envelope of the lower strata. Whirling dervishes, or the American Shakers, or Siberian Jumpers are based on such movements. And in this way they confirm to what an extent such forcible compressions of energy are inadmissible. The lower strata should not be surmounted with physical violence. The right way is through natural, spiritual ascent. Precisely the manifestation of Brotherhood assists such clearly beautiful ascent.

313. There could have been noticed extraordinary spatial currents of such tension that they overpowered mental sendings. This manifestation is rare, and the more should it be noted. Raging spatial currents do not continue for long, therefore it is very instructive to observe them. They cannot be prolonged, or they would produce a catastrophe. Equilibrium in itself can resist them, yet each such moment is dangerous. We call this the abyss of vortices.

314. Attentive observation is the more needed, for it is impossible to picture to oneself how an important manifestation can take place. Only a very refined organism can sense, as it were, a call; it will be desirous of making sudden observations. It is necessary to be prepared to respond to such a call.

315. It is not easy to gather together a brotherhood in full concordance. Let it be a group small in number, but without contradictions; it is easier for a small group both to convene and to separate. Any forcible bond is contrary to the concept of Brotherhood. Let them be only three, yet will their concordance be stronger than the vacillation of a hundred. Hesitation and confusion are injurious not only to people but also cosmically.

In olden times prolonged testings were designated in order to assemble a nucleus of the spiritually concordant. However, length of time alone does not solve the problem of selection. An evil seed can remain concealed for years and years. The feeling of the heart can whisper the better intimations. Too lightly do people handle a higher concept, and only a few know how to guard it with full love. Such cherishing is not in gesticulations and obeisances, but in indissoluble heart devotion. For some the bond will be fetters and chains, but for others it is a ladder of ascent.

The ignorant, those with overcast hearts, say, "Such a ladder is nebulous," because it is not for them to ascend. It is the more necessary to explain about Brotherhood, because soon people will seek cooperation. All encouragement for such cooperation will be needed. Thus, throughout the world respect for work will be manifested. Labor will be an antitoxin against gold. Yet, many times one is obliged to speak about the beauty of toil.

316. It is said that without stupidity Earth would be a paradise. It is a mistake to be consoled with thinking that nowadays there is less stupidity than in ancient times—at present it has become even more malignant. Each advanced stupidity is especially dangerous in playing with explosives. Stupidity does not think about the future. It is not disquieted by thought about epidemics. There are many kinds of new sicknesses, yet there will be still more of them. The manifestation of Brotherhood will be as ozone amid poisoned ruins.

317. An electrical apparatus produces discharges when energy is accumulated in it. There is no intention to shock certain people, but the discharge reaches those nearby. Likewise, a counterblow of psychic energy smites those who contact it with evil intent. The bearer of it does not wish to strike anyone, nevertheless the primary energy sends off discharges when a hostile force opposes it. Thus, the counterblow is not sent, but is evoked by the hostile force. Of course, where the primary energy is more powerful, the blow will be more crushing. It would be an inexcusable mistake to blame the bearer of the powerful energy for destroying someone. Not so, the assailant shatters himself.

318. Capacity for work must be cultivated, otherwise it will remain in a somnolent state. Also, capacity for work in the Subtle World must be developed. But the way to this must conform to the conditions of the Subtle World. There are many earthly means for approach to and realization of the Subtle World, but no forcible conventionality can create the best combinations with the Subtle World. As in all existence, natural realization of cooperation is needed. It may be fully realized or less realized, but straight-knowledge should be infused with it. Man should continually feel himself to be in the two worlds. I am not speaking about the expectancy of death, for death does not exist; I am speaking about labor, both earthly and subtle. Such assiduousness in subtle work should not tear one away from earthly labor, on the contrary, it will but improve its quality. Wrongfully, people do not think about the Subtle World; both asleep and awake they can take part mentally in the most uplifting tasks.

319. Being filled with lofty problems, man prepares himself for corresponding domains. By degrees he so accustoms himself to this way of thinking that he begins to belong entirely to an equally beautiful life in the Subtle World. Earthly life is an instant which has no co-measurement with the Higher World, therefore it is prudent even in this brief moment to derive advantage for the more prolonged one.

Brotherly cooperation brings one nearer to uplifting tasks.

320. The experienced swimmer springs from the heights into the depths of the water. He feels daring and joy at returning to the surface. So, too, the conscious spirit plunges into carnate matter, in order to rise again to the mountain heights. Experience makes such a testing joyful. Among earthly manifestations one needs to find comparisons with the higher worlds. The wayfarer likewise appears as a useful example. Compare the sensations of a wayfarer with proceeding through the Subtle World and you will receive a better analogy. Moreover, call to mind the different kinds of wayfarers and you receive a precise picture of the dwellers of the Subtle World. Some are afraid in general even to think about the way. Some dream about profit; some hasten to the assistance of a near one; some burn with malice; some seek knowledge. One can picture to oneself all the peculiarities of the wayfarers and decide for which of them the path will be easier.

321. In general, fearful wayfarers are not fitted for the path. Can one imagine a swimmer who is afraid of the water? Likewise harmful is fear before advancing into the Subtle World. Only steadfastness and aspiration to the Highest can further the ascent. He who strives toward something beloved does not count the steps of the ladder. Thus, it is necessary to love in order to attain.

Brotherhood teaches this means of ascent.

322. Standing on guard is a sign of broadened consciousness. Many do not understand at all what it means to guard that which is most precious. It is impossible to rely upon those who do not know about value. But one may rejoice at each wakeful sentinel.

Brotherhood teaches such a vigil.

323. Kriyasakti in all its inexhaustibleness has been known to people from time immemorial. I use the Hindu word to show how long ago people defined this energy with complete precision. Is it possible that present day thinkers will lag behind their forefathers? Right now thought-creativeness is found to be under such doubt that it is included in the humanities, whereas according to contemporary terminology, mental energy ought rather to be a part of the physical sciences. Thus, let those who assail thought-energy find themselves in the camp of the ignorant. Do not think that I am saying anything new; unfortunately, there are too few worthy cognizant ones, and as a result the most natural subjects are left in association with some sort of sorcery. Therefore it is indispensable to dispel superstition and ignorance.

324. It is especially difficult to help people involved in karma. It may be noticed that each good action encounters a certain counteraction from the one to whom help is sent. Thus is confirmed the ever-presence of the particular energy that is called the guardian of karma. Those who disturb karma, encounter, as it were, a repulse. Each one can recall how his useful counsels have occasioned a most inexplicable rebuff. People who were considered rational have sometimes begun to speak against their own advantage. One should then seek the reason in karmic causes. The guardian of karma is very strong.

325. The lightning of thought can sometimes be seen. The manifestation is rare, but when the energy of thought attains such tension, it should be highly valued. For the time being people may consider such a manifestation a fairy tale, but the time will come when the currents of thought will be investigated and measured.

326. People are always astonished at unexpected manifestations, but they forget how many invisible conditions are needed for each manifestation in the earthly strata.

327. The Himalayan lights have been observed by many scholars, nonetheless, for the ignorant they remain doubtful. The non-searing flame of the Himalayas, though people have observed and touched it, likewise remains as before within the limits of the fantastic. Each manifestation of light has energy in its basis, but such a force is denied. Even luminous stars and flashes seen by many are referred to ocular abnormalities. Actually, this poor interpretation is contradicted by the fact that such manifestations are simultaneously seen by several people. However, people do not usually inform each other about their sensations and visions. As a result much remains unnoticed. Therefore, the lightnings of thought also will be mere phantoms for the majority. Yet many animals are called electrical because they preserve within themselves a considerable store of energy; and similarly, certain people can be called electrical. Is it too difficult to imagine that their thought-energy can be visible as a brilliant flash, especially when a crossing of currents may be taking place? One should know how to keep one's eyes open. One must take the trouble to observe, otherwise many remarkable manifestations will pass unnoticed. The Himalayan lights furnish a suitable example.

328. The same tensions of energy also have curative properties. Thus, for example, the lightning of thought is very useful for the eyesight. But it is necessary not only to see it but also to realize the significance of this manifestation. In antiquity these lightnings were called foresight. Other manifestations of light can also have a curative significance.

329. We have spoken here about capacity for labor in the earthly world as well as in the Subtle. But capacity for labor alone is only a possibility for improvement. It is also required that one grow to love with one's whole heart the striving for subtle labor. It can be manifested each instant, and for it all other reflections should be set aside.

330. Frequently there occur fallacies about the names of energies. People cannot understand why the primary energy is called by different names. But there may be names which were given by different peoples. Moreover, the manifestation of different aspects of it has been identified by many definitives. It is impossible to establish a single designation for manifestations which are so very diverse. In the history of humanity it can be traced how attentively people have detected the subtlest shades of this same energy. It would seem that at present observations ought to be deepened, but in fact it proves to be almost the opposite. People are attempting to justify themselves by the complexity of life, but it is more accurate to explain this as aimless dispersion of thinking. The more should one repeat about the art of thinking. If it be not sufficiently developed in schools, then the family must come to its assistance. One should not allow man to become scatter-brained, that is to say, irresponsible.

331. Actually, calamities can turn humanity back to austere thinking. You have noticed more than once that great calamities have transformed a people. Affirmation of wholesome principles has come in thunder and lightning. Suffering leads to advancement. The ignorant cannot understand fiery purification, yet what can be more beautiful than this element when there is no fear! Thus, We often direct you to the Subtle World as the entryway to the Fiery World.

332. The indistinctness of subtle faces, which were seen, has its causes. The faces from the middle spheres can be irksome, and man encloses himself, as it were, in a protective network in order that these guests not fatigue him uselessly. In the Subtle World a similar demarcation of spheres can be noticed, otherwise a disorder would result that would be reflected in many ways.

333. It is undeniable that it is useful to provide oneself with clear thinking for the Subtle World. Only then is it possible to cross the great threshold in full consciousness.

334. It is possible to carry out many observations of radiations. It can be proven that over and above the radiations that are accessible even to photography, there exist still more subtle light waves that can be detected by a more refined apparatus. The effect of the waves spreads over great distances. Moreover, the possibility is explained of tearing away portions of the basic aura within the limits of subtle waves. Though it is rare, yet forceful people can see portions of their own auras. Such manifestations are rare because usually a man does not see his own radiation. It may be pointed out that such sendings of radiation are linked with thought-sendings. Thought, in passing through the aura, carries with it a portion thereof. Particles of the aura can be left on the interconnecting thread. Whoever sends many thoughts tears away a great number of particles from his aura. Therefore such mental labor is truly an achievement. Self-abnegation is also contained in that the pierced portions of the aura are easily subjected to the influence of opposed currents.

But the restoration of the tissue requires both time and the expenditure of energy.

Let no one conclude that it is proposed not to think in general; however, it must be kept in mind that each self-sacrificing expenditure of the aura calls forth a strengthening of the primary energy. Consequently in giving we receive.

335. Around the question of radiations are associated many considerations. The radiations of physicians and of all workers in fields of service should be studied with great care. A physician can carry away infection not only on his body and clothing but also in his radiation. If this has not yet been recorded, it does not mean that it does not exist. Similarly, the moods spread by certain people depend upon the quality of their radiation. In general, one should become accustomed to the fact that thought rules over the fate of man.

336. Sometimes one may feel, as it were, vibratory contacts on the skin in various parts of the body, but most of all in the region of the spine; it should be understood that this manifestation is also connected with thought transmission, especially when thought of great tension is under way. Such sensations do not usually draw attention to themselves, but nowadays when thought-energy is under discussion, the physical sensations connected with it ought to be observed especially. A thought that is sent is not always transformed into verbal forms by the recipients, but nonetheless it is imbedded in the mental apparatus and reacts upon the mode of thinking. Such an understanding of thought reception should be noted. Up to this time only thought translated into words has been taken into consideration, but the deepest reaction, beyond words, has remained without attention.

337. In this regard antiquity provides indicative

examples. People understood long ago that thought does not need words of a particular language. Mental energy strikes upon the brain apparatus and evokes a sounding understood by the consciousness. Whether such a sounding be composed of words or lies deeper in the consciousness is merely a detail. Through the method of thinking the chief understanding is precipitated.

338. In conceiving of Brotherhood the science of thought has enormous significance. When concordance is based, not on conventional agreement, but on heart cooperation, the manifestation of thought is especially intelligible and authoritative. One need not be surprised that the concept of Brotherhood requires so many consonances. These vibrations are joyful ones.

339. A dead pearl is revivified when worn by certain people. Only the presence of the primary energy can explain this natural process. One should observe similar manifestations in all the domains of life. It can be seen how long different objects last when used by certain people. It can be observed how animatedly the primary energy acts by its own strength when warmed by the fire of the heart. It can be seen how salutary certain people are, who do not even suspect the vivid presence of the primary energy in themselves. But if, in addition, they were to become conscious of their force, then their beneficent activity would be broadly increased.

One should not cut short even the least occurrence of the useful energy. No one has the right not to apply the smallest particle of usefulness for humanity. It is trickery to excuse one's own inaction with the pretext that there is someone else who is stronger. Very injurious is each evasion of self-sacrifice. One can revivify pearls without feeling tired; it is possible likewise to warm many hearts by feeling joy.

340. "Furious persecutors, whither are you driving us? Without being aware of it, you bring us nearer to the Refuge of Light." This ancient song can be repeated in all ages. In all tongues is it possible to confirm this truth, therefore it is better to be the pursued than the pursuer.

341. Thought is the law of the world. This law must be understood in all its fullness. Thought is not only verbal expression, the domain of thought is also the domain of mental energy. Precisely this circumstance is lost sight of, and only a small range is allotted for the diffusion of thought. Such limitation prevents from representing thought as beyond the limits of the planet, in other words, it deprives thought of its noble meaning. Thought, just as does thought-energy, actually assumes due significance when it is understood as existing beyond the limits of Earth. It is impossible to limit thought to the earthly sphere, otherwise radio waves could compete with this greatest of energies. Constricting the greatest energy also aids the belittlement of human thinking. Verily, the more man constrains his possibilities, the more does he cut himself off from great cooperation.

Thought should be studied in the best scientific institutions. Thought should be placed at the head of the physical conditions of life.

342. Prejudice is the entryway for injustice and ignorance. But people should recognize the boundary line of prejudice. This worm lives in the same house with doubt like a younger kinsman. A very keen eye is needed in order to discern such a dangerous mite. Each manifestation, each object, is usually encountered by people with varying degrees of prejudice. People try to justify themselves by saying that since they perceive objects they must as a preliminary measure preserve their unprejudiced judgment. But as a matter of fact, instead of impartiality they exhibit the most cruel prejudice. One should keep this popular weakness in mind in order to know from what to liberate oneself.

343. Prejudice is not fitting for Brotherhood.

344. Any belittlement of thought is not fitting for Brotherhood.

345. Any careless attitude toward a manifestation of the higher spheres is not fitting for Brotherhood.

346. Unity is the light-winged dream of humanity; when the dream approaches fulfillment, only a few followers remain. The transformation of intention into action drives the majority away. Thus, affirmation of unity is aspiration to the higher law, which humanity in its present state contains with difficulty. But each one who wishes to serve Brotherhood is not afraid of even the concepts most unaccepted by the majority; though striving for unity will be found only in exceptional consciousnesses. Each healthful place must be safeguarded. Thus will begin to come into being a healthy envelope of the planet. Right now it is greatly poisoned.

347. O, two-legged beings! Why do you so easily fall into a brutish condition?

348. The most ordinary eye can discern signs of the Subtle World. Frequently it is possible to see, as it were, certain color formations. It is amazing how something turbid actually swirls around some people, while at the same time others see quite clearly. Each one can recall cases when he rubbed his eyes after seeing something unexpected, and then as usual referred this sensation to some ailment of the eyes. It never entered his mind that the manifestation seen existed outside of his eyes and could be seen by many others.

349. In great storehouses many remarkable objects can be found, but experts and investigators sometimes prefer to search among small unknown repositories, and such quests yield irreplaceable discoveries. And so in everything, one should make broad surveys in order not to lose new and precious cooperation. It has already been pointed out that the hundred-thousandth one is bringing useful stones for the structure, yet it is inadmissible to jostle a burden-bearer on his difficult path. One should not suspect or upbraid him. The cement of the building should not set prematurely; likewise, wayfarers cannot make progress more quickly than their human strength permits. It is a special joy to see how the structure is being completed. Many would not believe that the local stones were sound enough; they formed their opinion through egoism. But the dawn will show where right judgment was.

Thus, not only in great storehouses but also in small repositories are found precious things.

350. No one can instantaneously transform his consciousness. Many extraneous conditions are required. Only in a sound structure will stones lie undisturbed by earthquakes. Each day we lay the foundation for a new structure.

Whoever can rejoice at each day's labor is on the way to Brotherhood.

351. Even in the purest air a sunbeam reveals dust. With the naked eye one sees this saturation. How much more then is it possible to observe by means of subtle eyesight. One can actually accustom oneself to the realization of the saturation of space. A poor consciousness is reconciled to an illusory emptiness, but from such emptiness is born emptiness of consciousness. Living in emptiness, people become irresponsible, yet any irresponsibility is falsehood. Life in falsehood is a cringing before darkness.

Let the most primitive microscope assist us in realizing that space is filled. It is amply full. It is instructive to observe how the tiniest micro-organisms are in contact with the Subtle World. The most intense conflict is taking place for the purification of space. These almost undetectable impacts lead to grave commotions. The microcosm contends with the Macrocosm. Such a confrontation sounds improbable, yet equally mysterious is the borderline between the manifested and chaos.

352. One may hear about lucky and unlucky signs from those who study the chemism of the luminaries. Actually, there cannot be fortune or misfortune for the whole world. Thus, it is vain to think that an unlucky day would plunge the entire world into inaction. Nevertheless, if the chemism is tensed and weighty, one should manifest caution. Observations and cautiousness can yield the best results. It is better to remain circumspect on a day of ill fortune than to lose sharp-sightedness on a fortunate day. Incorrect understanding of astrology has led to many afflictions. Let us not forget that the chemism of the luminaries cannot exert an equal influence on everything and everyone. On the heights, on the ocean, and under the earth there cannot be identical reactions to the chemism. The science of the influence of the luminaries will become great when it shall be assimilated without prejudice.

353. One should keep in mind that even the most salutary remedies can turn into harmful ones, depending upon the condition of the organism. For example, during irritation prescribed strophanthus may evince

poisonous properties. Strophanthus is a regulator of heart activity and is excellent during tension or fatigue, but not during anger or irritation. Likewise, other remedies are good when they conform to the condition of the organism.

354. Lunar reactions and the influence of sunspots long ago attracted the attention of the best scholars. But why do other, no less significant, manifestations remain neglected? Lunar manifestations such as somnambulism are extremely crude compared with the action of many rays and currents. Even those having refined organisms assimilate only with difficulty the fact that their inner sensations depend first of all upon spatial currents.

Among scientific discoveries, the statement that sunspots promote wars sounds strange. From the standpoint of scientific analysis would it not be better to say that sunspots engender human madness? Such a definition is far nearer the truth, for this chemism actually reacts upon the nervous system. In this let us not forget that such a chemical reaction is quite prolonged. It would be incautious to consider that a lessening of sunspots immediately does away with the chemism in space.

Likewise, the results of poison gases go on acting for a long time. It is senseless to think that it is possible to open a window and the poisons will evaporate. They are absorbed in the soil, in fabrics, and they unquestionably act upon the internal organs. Moreover, such reactions are so little felt that only future effects will attract attention. There is much poisoning!

355. Each one who is preparing poison for a brother is creating a terrible fate for himself.

356. Little by little people are beginning to understand that their sufferings are not accidental. People are beginning to reflect upon the destinies of entire nations. It is not easy for them to understand which deeds have been the decisive ones. Frequently the actions which are most diverse in their consequences are not easily recognized. Not a few undisclosed crimes remain in the world, nonetheless, this karma saturates the world.

357. Horrible is the world, because people do not wish to know about the supermundane worlds. People have repudiated Brotherhood, forgetting about cooperation and unity.

358. You have already heard about people for whom all waters are alike, all air is the same, all trees of one species are identical, even the faces of a people are alike—such inattentiveness is amazing. And these people, not being able to notice subtle changes in nature, are the more incapable of forming an opinion about that which is invisible to their eyes. It is necessary to reiterate stressfully about such low consciousnesses, for they have stentorian voices.

359. One should also pay attention to the irregularity of many manifestations. Many are amazed that even the motion of the planets suffers fluctuation, and yet science establishes this. Gradually the reasons for such unexplained manifestations will be revealed, and these reasons will be quite unexpected.

360. Transition from the subtle state into the mental calls to mind the change of the earthly body to the subtle one. Not often is it possible to observe the change of the subtle body to the mental. It is especially characteristic that the liberated one wonders what to do with the subtle body. It is not quickly dispersed, and therefore the astonishment at how and what awaits it is understandable. There can be manifestations of this envelope, there can be seizures of it; only the presence

of a strong spirit can assist in dissipating the shell without wanderings. Such roaming envelopes are not at all necessary. Vacillations of the consciousness and attachment to the carnate state create these attractions to the earthly sphere. But if a strong spirit can exhort the liberated one and quiet the shell being left behind, then the transition can be a natural one. Thus it has been in a cited case.

361. For certain nations Brotherhood is something so remote that they even avoid thinking about it. They ridicule those peoples of Asia by whom the concept of Brotherhood is still considered sacred. It is cause for rejoicing when, over and above human laws, concepts live on which are beautiful in their loftiness. When people can establish a steadfast union with the concept of Brotherhood, then it will be possible to look forward to the building of firm foundations. Let the heights of the Caucasus, Altai, and Himalayas be the abodes of the Beautiful Brotherhood.

362. Amid the intensified conflict let us affirm the concept of Brotherhood.

363. Just as there exist different states of the body, so are there different strata of thought and memory. If a sending has touched upon a stratum of subtle memory, then it is extremely difficult to transfer it into earthly strata. It is even possible to pronounce the words, but nevertheless they will immediately disappear. They will remain in a fold of the subtle memory and will be manifested only in special combinations of currents.

364. It is impossible to progress without realization of the three worlds. In this they must be accepted just as naturally as is the light of the sun. Many recite memorized words about the worlds, but do not admit them into their consciousness. One can imagine what a drama goes on when the blocked off particles of the worlds are not admitted to cooperation with congenial spheres! Rightly has it been said that man is his own jailer.

365. During the reception and sending of thought there can be noticed a series of manifestations that confirm the fact that thought is energy. Sometimes one's breathing feels stifled. Some explain that the reason for this lies in tensed attention. But for the observer it is especially important to note that the thought process is accompanied by physical sensations. Likewise, sometimes part of a received word drops out; such a manifestation will be an effect of spatial currents, in other words, an effect of energy. Similarly can be observed an increase of heartbeat and irregular pulsation that will also be the result of the influence of energy. There can also be noticed sharp changes of mood and of temperature that are evidences of the currents. Thus it is possible to trace to what an extent all thought processes are connected with physical manifestations. An analogy may be found in observation of radio waves.

For a long time humanity already has been getting accustomed to the recognition of thought, but how little does the realization of this primary law penetrate the broad masses. Wisely has it been said that ideas rule the world. Yet up to now people repeat this, but do not apply it to life.

366. Notice how swiftly certain words rush past. It need not be thought that this depends only upon the sender; seek the cause in chemical vortices, which you have already observed. Only with great patience is it possible to overcome such spatial conditions. But one may be assured that even such swift thoughts remain in the subtle memory.

367. Thought is lightning. A received thought frequently strikes luminous manifestations in us; it then increases the radiance of the chakras. Likewise, it may be understood that spinal vibrations are closely connected with the reception of thought. I am reminding about such a manifestation, because on the paths to Brotherhood the realization of the manifestation of thought is inevitably needed.

368. It is actually possible to sense, as it were, the expansion of an organ, or movement in the bell or in the solar plexus. The timid will say, "Better drive away all thoughts rather than admit such manifestations that border upon pain." We shall reply, "Just try to kill thought!"

369. During high tensions of currents one should be very careful of one's health. It need not be thought that this will be in contradiction to selflessness. The essence is to be found in making wise use of forces.

370. If there could be more confiding relationships between people, many scientific observations could be confirmed. Let us turn to the question of identical thoughts flashing out simultaneously in different corners of the world. So many accusations of plagiarism could be refuted! But right now we call this to mind in connection with the diffusion of thought. The springing up of identical thoughts, ideas, and images can convince one of the existence of thought-energy. This comparison may indicate atavism on the part of different peoples.

People often talk about an epidemic of images, and right now you can observe how nations have identical obtrusive ideas. The more identical the thoughts in space, the more powerfully can vortices of energy be formed. But do not think that in them is contained that salutary unity which We have repeatedly prescribed.

371. Terror of the extraordinary links people

together, both in the little and in the great. One is afraid to move away from a place, another fears manifestations of the Subtle World. Shock at contact with the Subtle World is understandable as a result of difference of vibrations, but it is difficult to understand why the majority of people are frightened at everything unusual. Each new rhythm exasperates people. When they reject something, seek the cause in fear or in a presentiment of increased rhythm. Not fitting for Brotherhood are such fears of the unusual.

372. People inquire if the envelopes left behind by the mental body can be seen? Not only can they be seen but they will be especially attracted to the earthly sphere. The subtle body is drawn to the earthly sphere if the mental body does not attract it to a higher sphere. It is entirely conceivable that a shell left behind by the mental body will be attracted to the earthly sphere. Such phantoms can be especially terrifying to certain people, because in them the rational principle will be absent. And for the shells themselves such wanderings are not useful; drawing near to the carnate stratum reinforces them and prevents their natural dissolution. But all such manifestations respond only to the lower and middle strata of the Subtle World. A lofty condition furthers the speediest decomposition of the abandoned vehicles. Thus when lofty consciousnesses help the one who is passing over, the envelope is immediately consumed. It is exactly the same as in cremation. The complete analogy should not be surprising.

373. Strong are the rays of Jupiter; they further the rapid diffusion of the forces of Uranus. In time people will discover methods of treatment by means of the rays of the luminaries. Since earthly light rays are curative, how much more powerful are the rays of the luminaries!

374. The envelope referred to was quickly decomposed because assistance was rendered. Such help can be exerted also by the subtle body while still in earthly life. But for this, first of all, absence of fear is essential in order to have complete self-possession in any sphere whatsoever. It is impossible to teach oneself such self-possession; it must be born from within the consciousness. Indeed, the experiences of life teach courage. It has been said, "Each coward will tremble so long as he does not find the diamond of courage."

375. People will wonder why at times a very important thought reaches one fleetingly, whereas ordinary communications arrive clearly. One should decide with caution whether something is important, which appears to be ordinary. Sometimes the most ordinary circumstance contains the solution of something important. Often a single word forewarns about something essential. Often man is cautioned against danger by a single exclamation. It is well if in this hasty word he hears the warning. There are many examples of people having remained deaf to the most urgent Indications. At the moment when misfortune is taking place they recall in a flash how help was offered them, but it is already too late. People usually think that equal help can be extended in all the stages of circumstances. But can a cure be expected when the organism is already disintegrating? It is impossible to grow a non-existent hand, it is impossible to reanimate an already dying brain. Many examples can be cited when people beseeched resuscitation of the dying. Such an attitude merely shows complete lack of understanding of how to deal with energies.

Meanwhile, people lose sight of the battle with the elements. If they do not see this battle, it does not exist for them. In the most tensed hours they are ready to occupy themselves with everyday conflicts, not caring that a terrible vortex may be sweeping over them. They prefer to busy themselves with everyday offenses, leaving to someone else the arrangement of all matters.

376. People will probably ask how speedily can thought act. Instantly, but it must be received with expectancy. One must know how to preserve this expectancy even amidst increased labor. It is inadmissible to forget such a possibility, even when one's whole being is striving into a beloved sphere. Readiness is true courage.

377. Each machine creates a particular psychology on the part of the worker. The rhythm of a machine is a strong indication of the structure of thinking. Therefore one should study the rhythm of different machines. It may be said that a machine is a sign of an existing condition. A machine worker should receive special intellectual cultivation in order not to fall under the influence of the machine's rhythm. Many will not comprehend what has been said and will think that such abstract reasoning has no meaning. It is time to discriminate where is abstraction, and where actuality.

378. Thought does not die away in space. Horizontally and vertically thought traverses space. There is no limit to its expansion. But nothing can remain in the same state. We know about the inviolability of thought, but apparently transmutation of it is taking place, and one needs to know into what the thought is being transmuted. It flows into pure fire. A beautiful circle results. From the fire arises energy—a creative thought—and through the earthly furnace this thought is again united with fire. The circle is closed, and renewed energy ascends regenerated for new labor. Such consummated cycles can be observed throughout the Universe. But the evolution of thought will be

especially sublime. Therefore, does not this realization of the value of thought impel man to intensify his thought-energy? Let each one apprehend what kind of thought will be especially creative. Let man weigh in his heart which thought is fitting for him. Thus a selection of values takes place.

379. In its essence Brotherhood is a school of thinking. Each act of the Brotherhood is in itself the expression of a thought useful to humanity. Each new consciousness will be welcomed by the Brotherhood and will find support in it.

It is right that simultaneously in different countries cooperation is being hailed; such a web will be worthy of the Mother of the World.

380. Be more, more daring, learn how to recognize the date!

381. In studying thought transmission, people usually allow an error to enter which leads to disappointment. They try immediately to transmit a thought to a definite person at a definite hour, whereas it is necessary as a preliminary to test one's own receptivity independent of a definite person. One should learn to discriminate as to which thought is manifested from without, and which has been conceived within. Such discernment is familiar to each one who has been accustomed to watch his process of thinking. Such exercises upon oneself refine one's attentiveness.

382. A hermit dwelling by a mountain stream was asked, "Does not the noise of the waterfall disturb you?" He replied, "On the contrary, it helps my hearing. Moreover, the stream reminds me of two concepts—consonance and continuity. I recall how people transgress their own paths. This variation in thoughts has the stream given me."

383. Is it not strange that the greatest truths do

not excite attention, whereas those of no consequence capture all striving? Do not people measure their own consciousnesses by these means? Who established laws of banality, and when?

384. Sometimes it may be noticed that the process of thought ceases, as it were. One should not assume a decline of energy. On the contrary, an outflow of energy is taking place, and it is so strong that the energy is working from within. Such circumstances must be taken into consideration. Of course, not only does the outflow of energy take place consciously but it also flows independently, bringing succor or raising a defense. Many conditions enter in during thought-sendings and processes. One must have a very open eye in order to perceive a sort of vortical cloud being carried along. Likewise, let us not forget that our consciousness is striving inwardly to render help to such an extent that the flesh is not even aware of this benefaction.

385. Reason is the guide of misunderstanding. Rational thinking is being condemned, but irrational actions have also been condemned. This means that there is some force that should supplement the action of the reason. The heart must be the supreme judge. Being the conscience of peoples, it will produce equilibrium. Reason is not equilibrium.

386. Contemporary knowledge of the qualities of the inner man must broaden its field, but this is still far off. Humanity must first be cleansed in the fire of testing.

387. The sensation of a protecting hand can be extremely real. It is not a symbol, but a manifestation of the precious energy.

388. Cooperative labor points out paths for new construction, but one should display sensitiveness to the manifestations of life. The manifestation of growth resounds broadly. Our Community does not use force, it practices voluntary cooperation. The manifestation of understanding prepares messengers of Light.

389. People are astonished at the existence of the Higher World. They do not wish to acknowledge its influence upon the events of earthly life. Events are accelerating. Vortices of happenings do not allow humanity to come to its senses. Man deems himself the creator of the New World. Contemporary leaders think that they are building the New World, but it enters no one's mind that their New World is a grimace of the old. The New World proceeds by new paths.

390. Striving toward the Light cannot be extinguished if a man is searching sincerely. We know the secret places of the spirit, and the froth of life will not stop Us. A temporary obscuration does not mean that a man has fallen off. It is necessary to know how to distinguish the character of these manifestations, their transitory nature; thus is it possible to discover and preserve useful people. Therefore Our selection is often surprising. The main thing is to distinguish the real from the superficial.

391. Let us find courage to meet dates; let us understand the chain of events; and in a threatening hour let us smile at news about achievement. It is twilight in the West. Madmen do not know upon what they infringe, and the ignorant affirm their superiority. It is better not to see the emanations of humanity. Darkness is overtaking those who have lost the path to Light.

392. The man who feels himself unlucky has been called an obscurer of the heavens. He has collected gloom around himself and has infected the distant space. He has harmed himself, but still more all that

exists. He has proved himself to be an egoist, forgetting about his surroundings. Depriving himself of good fortune, he has become a breeding ground of afflictions. As the self-satisfied one loses the thread of advance, so does he who is filled with self-pity cut away his own success. It is not fitting for man to doom himself to calamities. Long-sown wails and groans turn into a ruinous vortex. The itch of envy changes into leprosy; from malice the tongue grows numb. A whole hotbed of disasters is built by the man who gives himself over to the illusion of bad luck. Such poisoners are intolerable in the Brotherhood. Yet many dream about Brotherhood without thinking what a burden They bear! How strong is the man who realizes the good fortune of being a man!

393. During sendings of thought one should select sonorous and unusual words. Do not repeat them, and do not complicate the sending. One may repeat for explanation, but one should not repeat the same word with different meanings. The main consideration is that petty thoughts should not rise up, thus cutting through the basis of thinking. These small flies are difficult to exterminate; they also give a gray color to the radiation. Man assumes that no one and nothing interferes with his thoughts, yet at the same time his consciousness is full of tiny tadpoles, and his thinking turns into a quagmire.

394. The sound of words should be beautiful, such harmony also produces exalted thinking. It is inadmissible to disregard any means of uplifting the consciousness. Foul language, as an infection of space, brings debasement of the whole intellect. Ugliness in all its aspects is a dangerous malady. For humanity's sake one must understand where is cure and where dissolution. It is time to cognize the purification of earthly existence. It is inadmissible to disturb space with curses that unexpectedly smite innocent beings. An arrow loosed in a moving crowd can strike a blameless one. Likewise, during thinking one can strike where karma has prepared a weak spot. Perhaps, without such a blow, karma could have somehow been altered, yet the misfortune of the blow can smite undeservedly. Therefore, people must understand their responsibility for each word let loose.

395. Many think it not worth-while to be concerned about words and thoughts, for the world goes on in spite of curses. But such fools are blind, precisely, they do not see all the afflictions and misfortunes attracted by humanity. Let us not threaten, but advise purifying the atmosphere. Again large areas have been encompassed by violent commotions. Shocks may be expected. Not for long can people put off the results of their sowings.

396. Yogis are acquainted with attacks, as it were, of sudden drowsiness and fatigue, called the cloud of cognition. Indeed, the Yogi knows that at this time his energy is ebbing, attracted by the powerful flow of spatial current. The Yogi knows that he has taken part in Great Service for the good of humanity. It is possible to distinguish many aspects of such services. Sometimes only drowsiness is felt, but sometimes the subtle body strives to take part in an undeferrable action. Then one can see such a subtle body as a vision, or sense an invisible presence. The manifestation of such actions at a distance will be instantaneous. No earthly time is required for prolonged discourses and influences. When a Yogi feels the approach of a moment of drowsiness, he yields to such an imperative call, otherwise he may let pass an opportunity for cooperation in something great. It is especially indicative that those communions take place at remote distances and with persons absolutely unknown. Thus, the magnet of attraction is the more remarkable on the basis of thought-energy. Many manifestations may be noticed that are usually ignored.

397. The Yogi values many earthly oppressions which fall to his path. Each such suffering is called the hastened way. Sharpening of feelings cannot take place without overcoming obstacles. Therefore let us not scorn the accelerating paths.

398. After a separation the wise like to sit awhile in silence. In such a preface is expressed great experience. Let the radiations be settled and thought-energy be put in equilibrium. Each employment of energy should be sensible.

399. Pay attention to how much people turn away, falling under the influence of casual rumors. Their brains cease to work and become like a sponge left in dirty water.

400. Even the smallest signs lead to great manifestations, but people do not realize that a pathway overgrown with brambles can lead to a glorious achievement. It is the usual mistake to demand large earthly signs for advancing. One must understand the entire and most subtle fabric befitting the Greatest Image. One must not permit people to defame beautiful existence. Those Images must be brought to Earth which do not cause harmful confusion. As it is, the great Tree is cloven, its separate branches withered. It is not evident that anyone has regretted the scattering of the One Treasure. The foolish assume that discourse about the severed branches is a needless symbol, for they do not even know how to think about Oneness. These ignorant ones cannot understand the collective concept of Brotherhood. What is the dome to them, when they have not even laid the steps!

401. It is time to understand that the human path has been directed toward cooperation. No government will be enduring without affirmation of cooperation. This is no dream beyond the clouds, but the requirement for a date of evolution. Thus, let us not consider it an abstraction when the saving measure is proposed to us.

402. Who can take it upon himself to judge that which he does not know? Who presumes to affirm the presence or absence of something unknown? It is more sensible to admit that much exists which is unknown to people. Let people at times reread this simple truth.

403. Some appear as messengers, who have consciously and selflessly accepted the responsibility; others bear tidings without knowing it; a third group partially affirms a useful word; a fourth displays useful actions by the examples of their lives. There are many kinds of offerings and affirmations. Let us not designate which can be especially useful. Each one within his own horizon can direct people to good. Let us welcome each good offering. Courage enables one to array oneself in impenetrable armor.

404. Why does not a plea for help ring out when it is undeferrable? Help is the force of Brotherhood. It is impossible to compel people if they are not conscious of this undeferrableness. To him who does not wish to follow a path favorable for both himself and the Brotherhood all advices about the power of unity will be superfluous as long as he does not realize his complete error.

405. The manifestation of Wise Teachings enables one not to lose sight of the goal. An experienced archer sends the arrow firmly, but the hand of the faint-hearted trembles. The goal cannot be attained through errancy and staggering. Each belittlement of the Sublime fills the spirit with unsteadiness. The beautiful Sublimity is a shield against all errancy. Man goes straight to the Beautiful. He will not turn his back upon the Beautiful, nor will he utter disparagement of the Beautiful.

406. Unbelief does not belong to spiritual discussions only; it belongs to all domains of knowledge. A particular type of people is subject to unbelief. They deprive themselves of any creativeness; they cannot be inventors; they do not know inspiration. Such unbelievers can impede the movement of evolution. There are many of them, and they are capable of condemning everything not encompassed by their consciousness. Let us not take an example from these walking corpses.

407. And yet, how to deal with unbelievers who try everywhere to cause cleavages? There are very many of them, and owing to their ignorance they are very clamorous and meddlesome. One should muster a few scientific arguments against them. They cannot brook having the extreme irrelevancy of their opinions pointed out to them. Fortunately, science in different domains helps to illumine the paths of evolution. Of course, the ignorant will insist upon long outworn concepts. They do not like it when they are asked for proofs. Their attempts to screen themselves with scientific terms merely prove their narrowness of conception. Sometimes it is useful to come in touch with stagnation in order to perceive the entire extent of the obstacles to freedom of evolution. One need not be distressed at the existence of such branded consciousnesses. Each word which serves as a challenge to them will be a useful sowing. Let them even become abusive, nevertheless an agitation of matter will result.

408. Brotherhood teaches discernment of the boundary lines where it is possible to attain useful results. Many are already in such a state of corruption that instead of an agitation of matter only infection of space results. Each disciple of the Brotherhood understands where a contact is already impossible.

409. Tolerance is one of the conditions of observation. True observation is the basis of cognition. An intolerant man cannot form a just picture of things. He deprives himself of observation and loses perspicacity. What kind of cognition can be born from egoism which rejects reality? There are many examples of great truths having been subjected to distortion, because of intolerance. It may be said that intolerance is ignorance, but this definition will be too mild. Intolerance is evil; there can be no good intolerance. It invariably contains falsehood, because it conceals the truth. Only those who definitely lack intelligence can light-mindedly fail to consider intolerance as something unworthy.

410. It has already been said that the science of thought transmission at a distance is ordained as an attainment of humanity. However, it must be an authentic science and must arouse a respect worthy of it. It is inadmissible that people should respect a primitive apparatus more than the great energy contained within themselves. Do not think that an understanding of the forces concealed in man has been sufficiently strongly established. There is far too little respect for such forces among illiterate people. They are ready to hurl themselves into the dark abyss of so-called spiritualism, but they do not wish to reflect about the power contained in thoughts. The science of thought cannot be developed if people do not pay attention to it.

411. Be very cautious, for the currents are not natural. The sharp changes not only of temperature but also of chemism itself cannot be ordinary ones. There are such confusions throughout the world that it is more necessary to protect oneself, otherwise there can be derangement of the centers. Chemism can act as a poison. The manifestation of disorganization of interplanetary currents is too little studied. The air is considered to be as usual, just as are water and fire. But, then, do not these manifestations differ each instant?

412. Each arch has its apex. Disturbing it causes the downfall of the entire arch. Similarly there is in life the Highest Contact without which life turns into chaos. Is it easy to sense this point of Infinity? Few have sensed it, but because of this the manifestation of Infinity has forever illumined their consciousness. Great is the concept of the subtlest energies that uplift the consciousness. It is impossible to call them other than subtlest. Earthly apparatuses do not detect them. No one has seen them, but some have been convinced of their presence by an indescribable feeling. It would seem that earthly forces are forever separated from the subtlest domain, yet for all that our planet is on the eve of realizing the higher energies if humanity so desires. In this condition is contained the chief affirmation of the possibility, for each possibility can be rejected by the insanity of the will. But it is inadmissible that the highest point of the beautiful arch be destroyed by madness. Let each one recollect the best moments of his life. Is it possible that even a cruel heart will not be softened! Let each one sense in his own life the contact with the highest point of beautiful energies.

413. Picture to yourself how the subtlest energy

touches us. Such an arrow must pierce all space. Though words may not be found to express the unrepeatable sensation, yet it remains as the most immutable in all existence.

414. The man who retains within himself even one subtlest sensation becomes forever an unusual being.

415. Not only exceptions but the majority of people can attain a sensation of the subtlest energies. They have but to think about them.

416. Yes, yes, yes, the usual mistake is that even people who accept the subtlest energies picture their action incorrectly. The manifestation of the subtlest energies is imagined as something thunder-like and physically striking. It is impossible to explain to people that their earthly nature makes the subtlest energies almost mute and imperceptible. Of course, the inner reaction will be enormous, but few have the consciousness sufficiently prepared to perceive these higher Contacts. It must not be thought that it is possible to receive sendings from the distant worlds without preparation. One should not be distressed that the dual nature, the earthly and the subtle, is not easily manifested as one. One is again obliged to remember about earthly cooperation, an idea which is assimilated with difficulty. It often excites the lowest passions instead of rational labor. If cooperation is rarely found, even in small circles, then with how much more difficulty is the synthesis of subtlest energies assimilated! We speak, not to distress you, but to implant patience and striving.

417. It is especially inadmissible to strive to apply the subtlest energies for personal aims. Though the Higher Force communicates inner power to us, it is impermissible to forcibly apply the beautiful energy for personal interest and gain. Merely give entry to the beautiful Force, and much will be added.

418. The non-duplication of experiments with the subtlest energies often diverts the attention of scholars. But they forget that it is not the energy which is unrepeatable, but they themselves. Moreover, they do not know how to create duplicate conditions surrounding the experiments. Many times you have had occasion to note how different were the attendant circumstances. But even an eminently experienced scholar does not attach significance to very diverse conditions. First of all, he does not pay attention to his own mood; yet the condition of the nerve centers will be decisive for many experiments. Likewise overlooked is the quality of the co-workers taking part in the experiments. But even in antiquity, and later by the alchemists, the value of cooperation was well understood. They knew also about the significance of sex. They did not deny lunar reaction and the force of the planets. But at present, such elementary conditions are considered almost witchcraft. It is impossible to persuade people that they are the bearers of the answers to many things.

419. Among things overlooked we also find neglect of the quality of thinking. Not enough has been said about this power. For example, man does not pay attention to the fact that during amplified thinking he involuntarily sends his thought abroad. Verily, strong thinkers must be very careful. Their thought can be more easily seized in space. You already know about currents which, as in a tube, preserve a sent thought, but even such a special measure cannot always be effective.

420. It is possible to intercept telegrams; it is likewise possible to intercept thought. Thus, silence is no concealment of a secret.

421. Each one has a great many relations with completely unknown people. Also, his name is pronounced somewhere. Let us not forget that such distant contacts often have a greater significance than contact with our near ones. It may be noticed to what an extent remote information is reflected upon all the inner centers. But such an unquestionable circumstance almost fails to be taken into consideration. People assume that bodily contact is especially important. Let us not deny that the physical handclasp also has significance. But a thought, remote, unharmonized, can exert a very strong influence. No one can see these distant threads, but a refined consciousness feels them.

422. Is it not remarkable that in sleep the consciousness could trace an approaching onset of heart contractions? Likewise is it remarkable that by certain vibrations it is possible to avert a strong attack of pain. Much can be noticed.

423. Many will read about Brotherhood; many will discuss this subject—but will many apply in life the fundamentals of Brotherhood? Not reading, not conversations are needed, but gleams of brotherly relations. Likewise needed are experiments with the energy of thought; though they may not yield brilliant results, nevertheless they will fill space and help someone unknown. Let empty arguments be abandoned that something has not been successful. Today it did not succeed in order that tomorrow it may blossom more beautifully.

424. Moreover, it is necessary to understand the significance of mutual respect, which lies in the foundation of Brotherhood. It is necessary to recognize the deep meaning of reciprocity when forces are increased tenfold. Brother will not censure brother, for he knows that condemnation is dissolution. Wisely does a brother help at each turning of the path. Thus, cooperation is first of all a scientific action.

425. When we compare phases of growth of consciousness with scientific methods, we do not wish at all to desiccate beautiful sources, on the contrary, we wish to create steadfast effluxes of energy. Science must reinforce the paths to higher cognition. The time has drawn near when the ancient symbols of knowledge must be transformed into scientific formulas. Let us not demean such a process of clarifying thinking. Let us learn how to find allies in the most unexpected domains. Not enemies, but co-workers will acquire knowledge of all the forces of nature.

The evidence reminds about the depths of reality. Thus, instead of dissecting a living organism, let us assemble the unification of consciousness. Let people not call Us dreamers, for We are lovers of precise knowledge, as far as it can be precise.

426. A subject must be introduced in schools—the synthesis of the sciences. From it students will perceive how closely connected are many branches of learning. They will see how great is the circle of science! They will apprehend that each scientist is in contact with an entire series of scientific provinces. If he cannot be fully conversant with them, at least he must understand their problems. Through acquaintance with synthesis, students will be able to more consciously select their own scientific activity. Let us not forget that up to the present such choice has been extremely fortuitous, often resting upon vague family traditions. Likewise, the student passed helplessly through disconnected school subjects without understanding precisely why these subjects were necessary. In the study of languages it has not usually been pointed out what are the advantages of each one. Therefore, a dull attitude toward learning has so often been noticed. This has not been laziness, but simply lack of knowledge of the meaning and aim of the subject. Assuming that each scientific subject should have an attractive introduction, the synthesis of science will enlighten even the smallest consciousness and lead it toward labor. It should not be thought that such synthesis can be absorbed only at an adult age. Actually, in their early studies it is especially easy for children to assimilate broad views. Of course, the exposition of this synthesis must be attractive.

427. In fact, the beauty of synthesis will remain throughout life. Each investigator who devotes himself to even the least detail in the structure of the Universe arrives at it through the principle of breadth, and not through narrowness. Thus, cognition will be all-embracing. Verily, where burns the fire of knowledge, there has been ordained a luminous future.

428. Knowledge is the gateway to Brotherhood. Let us not be surprised that the establishment of Brotherhood begins with the synthesis of the sciences. Though each one master but one subject, nevertheless he will know how to render respect to the countless branches of knowledge. In such respect is born the understanding of Brotherhood.

429. Even in the course of a short human life there can be noted the disappearance and appearance of islands, the shifting of lakes and rivers, the death and birth of volcanoes. One can see a continual advance of some shorelines and the recession of others. No one can say that over several decades a marked alteration of the planet's crust does not take place. Now if, during a half-century, you take the recession of shores known to you and prolong it over the hundreds of millions of years of the planet's existence, you can see what enormous alterations could have taken place. Let people take note of these figures known to everyone and marvel at the change of conditions on the planet. Such evidences are very useful for unreasonable people. Even up to the present the most ancient periods are subject to suspicion, for people do not think about hundreds of millions of years; such calculations are prohibited by the distorters of ancient symbols. But the young generation should be made to confront the great problems. Motion will be the basis to start from. Let our planet, with its great motion, be converted into a small globe. Let us not be afraid of realizing ourselves to be in the vortex of Infinity. Then, too, the concept of Brotherhood will prove to be a steadfast anchor.

430. Someone says, "I know all this," but he is wrong. He does not know about the meaning of Brotherhood. He has not gauged the significance of the planet in calculating the centuries. He has not thought about the flow of the horizon. Thus, let him conscientiously acknowledge how little the most fundamental concepts have entered into life and thinking. Such realization will be the first pathway to Brotherhood.

431. Let people ask the Great Wayfarer, whence has run his path? He will make no reply, because he bears secret knowledge and he has learned when and to whom to transmit the entrusted Burden.

432. A certain settler built his house at the foot of a volcano. When he was asked why he exposed himself to such peril, he replied, "The difference is merely that I know about my danger, but you do not know what surrounds you." Great equilibrium must be found between tranquillity and the realization of danger. It is inadvisable to surround oneself with terrors, but neither is carelessness the solution.

433. For some reason birds are considered carefree, but they not only sense bad weather they also display more concern about dates for nesting and migration than people do. Goal-fitness has been excellently developed in all the kingdoms of nature. This quality is not always appreciated by people; they know too little of the past, and they do not wish to think about the future. For the most part, investigations of the past are casual, and therefore findings are heterogeneous. People usually limit themselves to quests of known places; they forget that life passes along the most unexpected paths, and its traces can be found unostensibly and unexpectedly. It is essential to preserve the writings of contemporaries, which in the course of time will help to find places already leveled to the ground.

434. There exist ancient repositories of which you have heard. The Brotherhood has preserved invaluable memorials of the most ancient times. There are people who have seen these many-storied repositories. By imitating the basic labors of the Brotherhood people may become united in useful cooperation. The Brotherhood is not a myth, and treading in its steps will be a decisive construction. It is not forbidden to copy anything lofty. In all Teachings it is proposed that one test oneself by comparison with the best and most difficult attainments. Placing before oneself a lofty task, it is possible to attain no small results. All dangers will prove to be amusing phantoms.

435. Earthly life has sometimes been called temporal. Verily, among other conditions, earthly life has no duration. Brotherhood directs thoughts to the far-off worlds.

436. Joint brotherly service can begin when mutual recrimination has been abandoned. Discussion is not condemnation. There may be brotherly actions which are not immediately understood. It is possible to make inquiries about reasons, but it is inadmissible, through ignorance, to utter condemnation which is like a sharp knife. Brothers so respect each other that they do not suspect unworthy action on the part of a brother; they comprehend any situation and ponder how to render assistance. In such cooperation there will be not the slightest compulsion. But mutual understanding is not born in an instant—a certain period is required to harmonize the centers. Therefore, in antiquity a certain time was set as a testing for newcomers. In the course of this period they could quit the Brotherhood without grave consequences. This period could be from three to seven years, but after that a betrayal would entail the most serious consequences. One must not look at this as cruelty, for he who runs away during a thunderstorm may be struck by lightning. The very speed of his flight only increases the danger.

437. However, not by danger or by terror, but by joy is Brotherhood maintained. In harmony grow superearthly feelings. Whoever has once experienced these exalting sensations already knows the Magnet of Brotherhood.

438. In any experiments one should not give way to excess. In general, excesses are inadmissible, they are contrary to equilibrium. Man, as a complete microcosm, must not violate equilibrium which is bestowed with such difficulty.

439. The psychic nature is individual in both people and animals. It is an error to attribute it to a single race or species. One may notice in certain peoples a leaning toward psychic manifestations, but this quality still does not explain strong manifestations in the case of certain individuals; it is the same in the animal world. Some will say, May not this be evidence of the disorderliness of some laws? Not at all. On the con-

trary, it merely proves the existence of laws over and above earthly reasoning. There are many questions which lead into error those who cannot think above earthly reasoning. People have become accustomed to think about fortuitous boundaries of nations, taking them for something immutable; likewise an entire people should think uniformly; a species of animals should have the same characteristics—yet life itself teaches one to perceive a great diversity. Man will be far happier when he discovers the thread of laws of the psychic nature.

440. If catastrophe threatens Earth, is it not absurd to write something down, to study, and to conserve? Only from an earthly point of view is it possible to arrive at such a premise. If Subtle World does not exist, why should we bother about the earthly one. But We are speaking about life, not about a handful of earth.

441. "We already know about everything." So say those who do not fulfill the fundamentals of life. Each one encounters this boasting about knowing everything, and each one may be struck by the ignorance of such noisy braggarts. One can but deplore such impudent assertions. Let these persons test their obvious ignorance upon themselves. In themselves they confirm whence come so many failures into the world. Let us not bother to repeat about the causes of misfortune.

442. Without any instructions people know how to care for a beloved object. They will resourcefully discover how to keep it in concealment. They will exert themselves not to break or damage a beloved thing. Someone has said that people are most competent at preserving stones and metals, less so with plants, still less with animals, and least of all with man. You can judge for yourself how just is such an understanding. Man is a most subtle organism, and yet the most cruel treatment falls to his lot. Let us not close our eyes to the fact that the so-called abolishment of corporal punishment is merely a screen for still greater cruelty. When will the abolition of spiritual persecutions finally come! When will people realize that the highest degree of torture is torment of the spirit! As long as they are not conscious of the Subtle World, humaneness will not be realized. Let us not be surprised that some people require the division of the higher worlds into many degrees. Rather, let people, including those who demand the most, understand at least the Subtle World, so that they may know how to enter it worthily. The division will be grasped afterwards when at least the first degree of Infinity shall have been comprehended.

443. Brotherhood, like a Magnet, attracts ready souls. The paths differ, but there is that inner chord that sounds and calls to unity. One can feel the most salutary vibrations, but only a few understand the significance of such healing manifestations. It is impossible to explain in words alone how this unification takes place. One must have a broadened consciousness in order to understand and gratefully receive the Help sent. Thus will man begin to discern how the higher energy draws near.

444. Who can say that the tension of the world is decreasing? On the contrary, it is seething, and people do not even know how to define that which is taking place.

445. Around the concept of forgiveness there is a great lack of understanding. One who has forgiven someone assumes that he has accomplished something out of the ordinary, whereas he has merely preserved his own karma from complications. The forgiven one thinks that all has been ended, but, of course, karma remains ahead of him. True, the forgiving one did not intervene in the karma of the forgiven one and thus has not made it more burdensome, but the very law of karma remains with both participants. The Lords of Karma can alter this to a certain extent if the fire of purification flashes out brightly, but such a flame cannot easily be set alight.

Great sacrifices have been performed for the kindling of the fire. One must revere the memory of such self-sacrificing deeds. Beauty lives on in such calls. Neither time nor human confusion can stifle the calls to self-sacrifice. The records of Brotherhood also tell about this same thing. It is beautiful that even now the concept that has existed throughout the ages is not forgotten.

Let us not reject even a little understanding of the supermundane path.

446. Some people write down the changes in their attitude toward their surroundings. Such notes are useful, for they induce one to ponder on the evolutionary movements which are taking place. Let us not be afraid of making mistakes in such observations. It may be that a casual mood arbitrarily colored an observation, but even through the superimposed colors, movement can still be felt. Precisely such movement, as a symbol of life, will guide man.

447. Among one's customs one must retain all those that contribute to the elevation of the spirit. Let us not uproot feelings which can yield most precious branches. Let us not cut away healthy shoots, for it is impossible to create in an instant something new and more beautiful.

448. Ordinary human sensations are often called something supernatural. A presentiment is quite natural, but as a result of superstition it is referred to the category of unusual agglomerations. A feeling does not deceive, but to sense it will be a certain attainment. Especially do people lose their wits when waves of different sensations simultaneously rush over them. Even trained observers cannot discriminate between contrasting feelings. One may spring up from a nearby neighbor, whereas another comes flying from beyond the distant mountains. Frequently, a nearby circumstance can interrupt very important distant currents. Let us not be distressed by the small when great calls may be hastening on. It is necessary to adjust one's feeling to the greater, knowing that it may arise. Especially when space is so tensed, one must keep one's attention fixed upon the larger tasks.

449. A presentiment is sometimes called the figurehead of the ship. It runs in advance and does not allow itself to be overtaken. The new consciousness understands that the ship has a bow and a stern, but superstition adds to the bow of the ship the most fantastic image. Similarly, human thinking adorns the simplest sensations with unheard of forms.

450. Wherein, then, is progress? Some assume that it is in constant recognition of the new. Will not such aspiration be one-sided, and must there not be added to it regulation of the old? More than once it has been shown that people abstractly strive toward something new, and yet continue to dwell in an old pigsty. Someone gives lectures about cleanliness, yet is himself extremely filthy. Will such instruction be convincing? Or a lazy man summons to labor, but who will give heed to him? Let us not be afraid to repeat such primitive examples, for life is full of them.

Whoever thinks about harmony knows that a house is not new where old rubbish has settled. And yet one can see how beautiful attainments wither because they cannot grow in filth. Not only is such a fate of useful attainments deplorable to see but it is sad that their dissolution litters the already discovered paths for so long a time. This is why I speak about equilibrium.

451. Do not permit any quest to be traduced if it is sincere and has a good basis. Solicitude and care are necessary. As a gardener grows new fruit and fertilizes the soil, so let us be ready to assist the new and regulate the old. Whoever wishes to help must be prepared to assist in every way. Only with such readiness can one find the path of application.

452. Observe and if possible write down the dates of events. Later on, a remarkable mosaic can be put together.

453. As I have spoken about the relationship of the new to the old, so do I also speak about the correlation of the inner to the outer. Formerly, people were taught lying and hypocrisy and received praise for insincerity, but now such subjects have been abolished, for these qualities have become innate. Actually, it is necessary to pay attention to the tragic discord between the inner and the outer. Is it possible to expect special mastery of the lofty energy in such destructive disharmony? People are reaching such a degree of torpor that they cannot even imagine that man can bear within himself both enemy and friend in continuous conflict. It is impossible to possess power when on the face is a mask and in the heart, a dagger. Impossible is successful growth if the entire organism finds itself in a constant state of disunity. We have spoken about unity in order that each one shall understand it, not only in relation to his near ones, but also in regard to himself. Such inner disunity is in itself dissolutive and self-devouring.

In the discourses about Brotherhood, it is not

without reason that unity is so often called to mind. The meaning of this quality must be profoundly understood.

454. Each one has noticed with surprise that in the best Teachings schism has taken place. Certain leaders have even considered such occurrences useful for arousing discussion. But it must be contemplated that around the Truth there can be no contradictions. Only the blind do not see what stands before them. Will not the cause of such blindness be one's own disunity?

455. The history of various senseless disputes can serve as an edifying lesson. Throughout the world these follies are being perpetrated. Is it not timely to remind about Brotherhood?

456. Not only nonconformity of old and new, of inner and outer but also different understanding of the simplest words is an obstacle to the consolidation of progress. Do not consider it strange when the simplest concepts are wrongly interpreted—there exists no unity of consciousness. In spite of beautiful solitary flights people will bog down in one swamp in the majority of cases. It is impossible to instruct them in the higher energies when their very way of life needs regulation. You have heard about a disastrous termination of an experiment with currents of high tension, and you have rightly understood that the cause lay in carelessness. The first success not only did not inculcate carefulness but, on the contrary, admitted negligence. There are many such examples. Often it is impossible to bestow success, because it proves to be a dangerous plaything in foolish hands.

Much ignorance interrupts the paths of progress.

457. A mission, in itself, likewise bears danger. One must hold fast to one's mission, for hands are stretching out on all sides. Therefore it is not surprising that there are so many admonitions on the paths to Brotherhood. Whoever considers these exhortations superfluous is foolish. Who can boast that his traveling bag is in order?

458. About preparations for Brotherhood the simple truth must be understood—the more, the better. Let us not think that there is enough of everything. One must accept as an essential procedure the review of all things taken along. One should not take much, but it is inadmissible to forget what is needed. The selection itself will be an adequate test.

459. Thirst is slaked by water. Thirst for knowledge is slaked by the path of approach to the Higher World. Many scholars suffer their whole lives from indescribable anguish, because they alienate themselves from cognition of the Higher World. The anguish of the wrong path is most cruel, most devouring! In the end such a man finally abrogates his progress and is in torture without understanding his own error. Much malice is engendered by such beings. They are ready to persecute even the least manifestation of Light.

460. There are many human masks, but one of the most repulsive is the guise of unity. One has to sink into slime to dare such falsehood, to display the smile of unity when in the depths of the heart there hides a grimace of malice. One has to imagine a complete shattering of the spirit in order to understand to what an extent such a man violates human dignity.

Such an ugly manifestation takes place often, and how far removed it is from Brotherhood!

461. The Brotherhood is not a shelter, but a Beacon of Light, it is as a Watchtower; thus must the manifestation of the Brotherhood be understood. Otherwise, people will often assume that Brothers seek safety from various persecutors. No, the seclusion of the Brotherhood is necessitated by completely other causes. As a Beacon on a lofty peak, the Brotherhood applies its knowledge for the salvation of humanity.

462. Certain Teachers have advised against touching upon insoluble questions. Of course, they had in mind not rousing unprepared minds to resentment, but where discussion is possible, the most far-reaching intellectual excursions should be encouraged. Beauty sparks in prognoses which can come to life in brotherly unity.

463. It will be pointed out that many Communities and Brotherhoods have fallen into ruin, but they are not the ones We speak about. Moreover, they could have been moved elsewhere, but to a stranger's eye it might seem that they disintegrated. Do people know much about life in a neighboring house, much less about that which they are not supposed to know? Each one can recall from his own life the most significant events about which no one has known. Especially if transmitted by thought at a distance, who could learn about them? True, thought can be intercepted, but for this special conditions are necessary. If a thought has been directed with especial clarity to a definite person, it will unfailingly contact his aura. Thus communities can be kept together by the force of thought. But some are so afraid of thought that they decline everything relating to this domain. Such people should not be attracted, their approach ends in treachery. More than once Communities have been moved away in order to free them from undesirable people. It is easier to announce the dissolution of a Community than to disclose those who can do harm. From such a situation one can more easily comprehend why the Brotherhood is to be found in an inaccessible place. Therefore, too, each one who knows about the Brotherhood will be careful in giving out his information. People cannot bear it when they are unable to understand something. Such understandings are stratified slowly. Very rarely is the Chalice filled to overflowing. As a synthesized center, the Chalice preserves the most essential, indescribable accumulations.

464. The Chalice, just as the heart, is especially close to the concept of Brotherhood. The Chalice is the repository of everything loved and precious. Sometimes, much that has been gathered into the Chalice remains concealed for entire lives, but if the concept of Brotherhood has been impressed upon the Chalice, it will resound in both joy and yearning in all lives. To people who are cognizant of it even in an hour of difficulties and clashes, the concept of Brotherhood will be a saving factor.

465. Predisposed observers discern only their own preconceived design in actions and reactions. If all the distorted facts be called to mind, it will be horrifying to learn how many already discovered attainments have been destroyed. It is impossible to show any advance which has not been sullied by premeditated trickery! There are many causes for premeditation—the first will be ignorance, then come malice, envy, aversion to someone's success, dislike for the new—thus, many ignominious qualities distort the facts. In such a frame of mind is it easy to proceed with the cognition of the great energy?

At each step are encountered misunderstanding and malevolence. One has to have special cultivation of the will in order to accept these obstacles as unavoidable. But even though a man shall find in himself sufficient firmness to overcome such difficulties, still, so many most fortunate confluences of energies will be lost.

466. It is impossible to understand why even the

simplest observations are overlooked. For example, in studying aromas insufficient attention is paid to the usefulness or harmfulness of different very pleasant odors. All flowers have a particular designation, yet so-called perfumes bear conventional floral names. No one is concerned about the usefulness of the perfumes, but the essences used to make them up are sometimes almost poisonous. It is regrettable what the teaching about color and aroma has turned into when people propose to use arsenic coloring or deadly aroma!

467. Broad usefulness will be the adornment of the cooperative. Let nothing pernicious be admitted under any covering. Thus, let us draw near to the concept of Brotherhood.

Let us keep in mind that the most difficult hour can be the threshold of new achievement.

468. Always remember about the young co-workers. Remember that it is always possible to find them. Remember that they await you, even under diverse garments. Under a vague aspiration they are still ready to receive a word about new attainment. Through all the domains of science let a call be heard to the spacious truth. Let each one, though it be through physical culture, begin to think about culture of the spirit. Let biology remind one about unending life. If someone likes outlandish words, make no objections, for the paths are infinite. If someone is bewildered, encourage him, because not seldom is perplexity a sign of a secret thought. When someone views things with gloom is this not a sign of frustrated hope? One word about Infinity can bestow wings. When someone is silent, perhaps he is searching for the most expressive word—encourage him with a look. Many bridges can be enumerated by which young friends can cross over the stream. But the main thing remains that the readiness of young forces is great. This must be remembered by all who shake their heads in unbelief.

469. Concerning youth, it is necessary to make arrangements for each one who has chosen the brotherly path. It is needful that this inexhaustible source continually strengthen forces through reciprocity. Let us not think that only after a certain age youth becomes receptive. Memory frequently awakens quite early, and it is amazing how brilliantly thought is at work at a very early age.

470. The consciousness of adults sometimes dies away for a certain time, whereas children are acutely perceptive of precious qualities. Adults often fail to resound to the concept of heroism, but children are fond of popular heroes; they are enraptured by great deeds, and they dream of seeing themselves among the champions of the truth. It is inadmissible to deprive children of this living source of inspiration, which will remain a luminous glow throughout their lives. This aspiration is not sensuousness, but the growth of consciousness which has come in contact with a beautiful image. It is necessary to preserve by all means such contacts; from them is born also the concept of Brotherhood.

It should not be thought that the realization of Brotherhood comes from any sort of dogmatic moralizing. A beautiful achievement can illumine a young heart forever.

471. The happiness of the Teacher is in encouraging the disciples to dare toward Beauty. Long lists of tedious, torpid incidents do not promote this achievement. The Teacher himself must carry the flame and by his presence alone impart the fire. Such an everyday task is difficult, yet people are tested precisely in everyday life, which is the sister of Infinity.

472. An outflow of psychic energy is not at all susceptible to treatment by blood transfusion, but by valerian, musk, and milk with bicarbonate of soda. These basic remedies are supplemented by the psychic energy of the physician—the latter is quite essential. Our young friend possesses an excellent quality—he can give away a large quantity of energy without injuring himself, for there is none of that malice in him which usually has an enfeebling effect. Malice can produce a strong convulsion, therefore the basis of malice is not suitable.

473. Anemia is usually considered to be a blood deficiency, but this factor is not of fundamental importance. It is but a result of an outflow of psychic energy. Thoughtless physicians assume that it is possible to restore strength by drinking blood, but they forget that the inflow of strength will be one of appearance only. It is the same as trying to illumine a large house with a single match. Taking in blood produces much harm; this substance requires study and adaptation. That is why We do not in general advise such mixing of blood. Essentially, it is unnecessary. Increase in psychic energy is attained by the simple expedients of which We have already spoken. But in this let us see to it that there be not found in the vicinity someone who absorbs the energy. Indeed, it can be absorbed consciously and unconsciously. Each irritation, each despondency will definitely absorb the precious energy. When the fundamentals of Brotherhood are being taught, first to be eliminated are all those elements which are adverse to psychic energy.

474. It is advisable to observe the methods of the invasion of chaos. Many suppose that the very concept of chaos excludes any system. A representation of chaos as completely formless will be untrue. Even in each life it can be observed how subtly chaos creeps in. It intrudes as an actual decomposing force. "The Invasion of Chaos" could be the title of an extremely instructive book of observations.

475. Spatial voices have been mentioned under various names in the Scriptures of all peoples. Let us not delve into why such voices have been attributed to the most diverse sources. Right now it merely needs to be kept in mind that knowledge of these voices goes back to remote antiquity. One should not assume that people of the most diverse cultures could be mistaken or be intentional liars. Science has already mastered wireless transmission, which is being continually improved. Moreover, thoughts are being studied, and remarkable observations are already resulting, but for all that, ignorance has so greatly increased that it is necessary to reiterate even the simplest truths.

476. Not only are opinions and ideas about it not admitted but people even consider it harmful for the health to think about the primary energy. Even such absurd arguments exist. Such objectors do not admit that thoughts can not be harmful for the health, and consequently everything concerning thought can not be harmful. I affirm that thought is the natural principle of life. Nothing around this principle can be injurious; thoughtlessness is far more frightful.

477. Everyone has noticed certain people who ask very complicated questions and yet do not apply even the simplest fundamentals in their lives. Such incongruity is a poor sign. Would it not be better for them to apply the refined formulas in life? Such incongruities are to be cast off first of all on the path to Brotherhood.

478. Spatial calls reach Earth through the most unexpected receptions. An imperative call about altruism and mutual understanding reaches certain people. But pay attention to the unexpectedness of such arrivals. If, on a map of the world, the places be marked where Our call is perceived, a very unexpected pattern will result. But there are people to be found who repeat this very same thing without any understanding. Sometimes the sowers of dissension are not averse to speaking about altruism. The very meaning of the word is annulled, and instead of mutual understanding violent hatred emerges. But over and above all obstacles remains the call for altruism and mutual understanding. What is not understood today will come tomorrow.

479. People cannot understand by what signs to appraise actions. Here is an opinion brilliantly expressed, yet in the Higher valuation it is not considered very good. On the other hand, an opinion hesitantly voiced, full of modest reserve, deserves joyful commendation. To a superficial observer such an appraisal is not comprehensible. There can be brilliance in false stones. Deep thinking can also be expressed in very singular words. Where there is more inner glow, there must also be encouragement. When I speak about simplicity, I have in mind direct persuasiveness. When there is talk about raising the people's level, precisely simplicity is required in all its convincingness. This quality must not only be accepted with one's mind but loved with one's heart; from it emanate both cooperation and Brotherhood.

480. Dissonance is more audible than consonance. When one listens to the lower superearthly sphere, one may be staggered by the tortured groans, wails, and cries of terror. After these moans the succeeding spheres seem silent, but this impression is a relative one. The music of the spheres is sublime, but it does not harrow the nerve centers. So, too, in all that exists people are attracted by dissonance, but only a few know how to recognize concordance. On the paths to Brotherhood one must cognize the power of concordance.

481. Those who blaspheme against that which exists hope that their evil projections will go unpunished; they attempt to advance on the path of evil and boastfully assert that no arrow of justice will overtake them. Can one place reliance upon that which has not yet been manifested? Their thought attempts to hold it back, for the reason finds examples of immunity to punishment. But let them remember how short-sighted is reason.

482. Note to what extent even excellent people can be blinded! It is true that they cannot even perceive forewarnings. It is necessary to be extremely careful in cautioning them. One has to give such a warning in parts, not depending upon their eyes being opened at the very beginning.

483. In ancient communities each one undergoing testing was hailed. He was dealt with solicitously since it was known that it was inadmissible to forcibly interrupt the process of his experience. It was considered that each testing is a threshold to progress. No one could twist the path of effects, but brotherly encouragement enabled him not to slacken his pace, even before the most frightful images. Of course, chaos in its terrible ugliness inevitably tries to impede the path of each one being tested. But let these images be dreadful; the manifestation of the most horrible one will be in itself the forerunner of the end of the test.

484. Disciple, when you choose a most restricted sphere, still leave an hour for the all-encompassing. One cannot breathe in a straitened sphere, but even a small ray of Infinity will provide enough prana. All-encompassment exists in Infinity. When this truth is realized, then there exists no narrow and stifling sphere. In the quest for Brotherhood one must keep in mind these guideposts on the path of liberation.

485. When a great light draws near to someone's eyes, he exclaims, There is not enough light! Must not the cause be sought in blindness? Many examples can be cited when faulty eyes failed to see the light. Insensitiveness to light does not depend upon the light itself, but lies in poor eyesight. People who have eyes obstructed by dust can often be reminded of this. Can such a person be fit for the path to Brotherhood?

486. For the demonstration of concepts let us represent them graphically. Let us imagine unity in the aspect of a beautiful and stable dome. Let the threads of the elevation extend upward and be joined together as the facets of the dome. No one could suspect that unity could infringe upon individuality. With the ancient builders each column, each step was individual, yet none the less they went to make up the general harmony of the structure. The vault was held up, not by ornaments, but by correct internal cohesion—thus unity can be expected where that inner cohesion which rises to the Summit is understood. Let us not weary of collecting the best images around the concept of unity. Unity is so very necessary, and it is so often impaired even among those who already know about Brotherhood.

487. Leave behind all regrets about the past, let us not make the path to the future difficult for ourselves. The very mistakes of the past must not fix attention upon themselves. Striving into the future must be so strong that the light will not grow dim in eyes which are not directed backwards. Let us forsake the past for the sake of the future. One can strive so strongly into the future that in all conditions this blessed eagerness will forever remain. Each striving toward the future is striving toward Brotherhood.

488. It is necessary to understand how many external conditions go to make up man's frame of mind. This swarm is called "locusts."

489. Many have heard about the Kumaras, but few have rightly understood about them. This manifestation is something superearthly—thus do people say, but they forget with what labor the attainment is built. Scholars are already beginning to understand how a human personality enters into the pantheon of heroes. By the same path also are the qualities of the Leaders of humanity accumulated. If they do not pass through earthly sufferings, they cannot respond to people's sufferings. If they do not experience the sweat of toil, they cannot guide people in their labor. Self-abnegation, mercy, compassion, courage are forged in life. Nothing abstract can mold the strength of the spirit. Thus let people understand the Kumaras as the true Leaders.

490. The rhythm of battle lies not in a desire to kill. I affirm that manifested forces do not go out to fight; they stand on the defensive against chaos. Thus it is not easy for many to understand that the battle is continuous, only its rhythm changes. Timid ones tremble at a single mention of the battle and ask, When will it end? But they become completely crestfallen when told that the battle will come to an end only with the termination of chaos. Is this not terrifying for some? But terror is not suitable on the path to Brotherhood.

491. The Teacher bent his head over a cistern and asked the disciple, "What do you see?" The latter replied, "I see thy clear reflection." Then the Teacher directed, "Stir the surface with the little finger—what do you see?" "I see thy features distorted." "Think, if the touch of your little finger so altered my features seen in the water, what distortions will take place in the midst of subtle energies at a coarse contact?" In the smallest examples one can see what is also taking place in the Subtle World.

492. A great number of cells of the organism are to be found in a dormant state. It has been pointed out that their awakening would make a man luminous and able to fly. Is it conceivable that people in their present state could achieve such an awakening of light within themselves? Reflect that people are fully equipped for the furthermost evolution, but the treasure must be left asleep. The state of consciousness does not permit rapid advance. Only in rare cases is an organism illumined and, with help from the Subtle World, temporarily realizes the preordained possibilities.

493. On the path to Brotherhood one must lose the habit of belittlement. Why touch upon manifestations which the consciousness cannot yet accept? Let no injury take place, even through ignorance.

494. Do not think that one's own thoughts can have a preponderant influence upon dreams. Remote spatial thoughts can also produce such influences. The perception of distant thoughts is very easy during sleep. Dreams must be studied still further.

495. The Teacher has more than once exclaimed, "Joy!" But the disciples have looked around in perplexity, asking, "Where is this joy? The sky is beclouded and there is sorrow everywhere." Yet the Teacher has foreseen joy over and above the temporary frame of mind.

496. The Teacher has more than once forewarned of danger, but the disciples were astonished, Whence will danger break out amid peace and quiet? The Teacher already sensed where there could be the engendering of danger. Let us not be intimidated by danger, but let us encounter it vigilantly. Likewise with joy—let us not cast work aside, let us not lay down our task, but let us strengthen its quality through joy.

497. Those who seek Brotherhood belong to the fiery element. From Fire is born exaltation and inspiration. The luminous element may be revealed in each sigh about Brotherhood.

498. Even terrible criminals have been called "magnificent" because of their appreciation of beauty. Throughout the history of humanity one may find convincing proofs of beauty having been a shield. Constriction of creativeness is a sign of a decline of humanity, whereas each epoch of the renaissance of creative power remained as a step of achievement. Since this is widely known, why is art not applied in life? It may be recalled that beautiful monuments to creativeness have become manifest as salutary landmarks; in striving, people have hastened to them, for they bore peace.

Without beauty one cannot think about Brotherhood.

499. Let us talk about motion. Misunderstandings continue to be piled around this concept. Hearing about motion and mobility, people turn into restless runners. But can bustle be fitting for higher manifestations? Similarly, people do not distinguish outer from inner movement, yet such a distinction is quite essential; it saves one from bustle, which unavoidably leads to falsehood.

Likewise, understanding of inner motion will bestow dignity of movement. Gestures and movement itself are not easily acquired by people; often they do not know how to handle their hands, feet, and even their heads. The head shakes, the hands wave about, the feet stumble—really, must one even teach them how to walk? However, all these blunderings are due to disorderliness of consciousness. Aimless bustling is an expression of a lack of adaptability to life. It is not fitting to be a buffoon on the path to Brotherhood.

Thus, let us learn to distinguish an inner movement from an outer one.

500. Likewise, let us not weary of repeating about unity; in this concept there is a constant intermixture of the inner with the outer. People will say, We are in unity, there exist but small crevices; but they forget that crevices are the seat of decay. Thus, they do not attach significance to inner unity. Yet, what edicts can implant the signs of harmony? It but remains to appeal to humanity's sense of shame. But without an understanding of harmony there can be no Brotherhood.

501. One should also reiterate about peace. Let the word itself follow people on all paths.

502. Can there be any judgment concerning peace among those who are full of coarseness and cruelty? One should observe such peacemakers in their daily home life. One should hear how they discuss their own affairs and those of others. One ought to become acquainted with their jokes and slanders in order to understand their complete unfitness in the matter of peace. But no one is concerned with the moral level of those who sit in judgment on the destinies of whole nations. No one will reflect that nothing clean comes out of dirt.

503. Fury—thus is called that horrible state into which fall those possessed by egoism, and who approach the higher Teachings for the sake of gain. Their condition cannot be called other than fury. Let physicians examine their saliva to be convinced of the pathological state of their organisms. Someone may ask, Do they bite? He will be right, for their touch is poisonous. One may name many examples of this madness. It is amazing with what dark intentions such people approach the Sources of Light. It is shocking to realize that man rushes into a hideous abyss without looking ahead further than today.

504. Where, then, in earthly existence should one seek the flashes of Brotherhood? Signs of it may be found among very simple workers who have come to love their work. Labor, love, and brotherhood dwell together.

505. A union organized as a limited partnership requires a very succinct statute, but the Brotherhood cannot have a written code. Brotherhood cannot be maintained by a stipulated constraint. The very word limitation is out of place in the boundlessness of Brotherhood.

Whoever understands Brotherhood as a yoke, let him speedily depart. Whoever bows dejectedly before the Gates of Brotherhood, let him quickly turn back. To be able to rejoice at Brotherhood will indeed be a wise joy.

506. Wise joy will be manifested also at ordained encounters. Not often do people sense when their encounters have deep roots. Vivid recollections sparkle like instantaneous flashes. At times they produce an unpleasant confusion, as if they were not to be admitted into the ways of everyday life. Therefore, it is necessary to analyze one's impressions cautiously. Besides the veracity of one's first impression there may be various recollections. Sometimes, even good people may not appear in their higher aspect. I mention this so that you may avoid too hasty a judgment. You have already been convinced of how often friends could mistake casual aspects for the fundamental ones.

507. In dreams there sometimes appear clearly

defined faces of complete strangers, whom one meets later on in life. There are many explanations for such prevision, but first of all, it becomes clear that by some sort of sight man perceives that which he will see later in the physical aspect. Indeed, these encounters bear witness to the Subtle World and to activity in it during sleep. But these deductions do not enter the minds of those who investigate the domain of dreams. It is especially noteworthy that such previsioned encounters often prove to be unimportant in the physical body. This circumstance proves that actions in the Subtle World operate differently from those in the physical one. It is a cause for rejoicing that even by visual examples one may see how heterogeneous is the life of man.

508. Spatial currents also are not something abstract. They influence not only the condition of man but even the radio waves. Even in aviation certain strange manifestations can be observed that can be explained only by the currents of space. Thus, let us note each bit of evidence about subtle energies.

One must have an open and free eye on the path to Brotherhood. When, for some reason, a distant response does not arrive, one must always give thought to the many causes. Aside from the reasons that lie in the communicants themselves, there can be great spatial causes. Currents can be so intensified that it may be necessary to wait for a change so that the transmission can be accomplished.

509. In the East people thought about a Northern Shambhala, which manifested as the aurora borealis. There also existed a legend that a banner would be set up at the point of the North Pole. Thus are traditions fulfilled; and one may glance into the distant future when, through a shifting of the terrestrial axis, new lands will be discovered which are now concealed. I have already spoken about the uncovering of the tundras. I commend those who look into the future.

510. In ancient epochs the meaning of life was understood more profoundly than at present. All the remarkable contemporary discoveries not only have not focused attention upon the fundamental meaning of life but they have often led away the thought even into the realm of mechanics. Efforts must be exerted to direct thought to the very basis of existence. The level of thinking of ancient philosophers should be compared with the trend of the reasonings of contemporary scientists. Aside from knowledge of many scientific discoveries, the philosophers of antiquity often knew how to present very profound formulas of life. It is essential that the art of thinking again rise above the external conditions, which are subordinate factors of existence.

511. Does man know the dimensions of his actions? Can man determine the inception of good or evil caused by his actions, so long as human thinking remains in earthly shackles? Verily, man does not know the scope of what he creates. Only thought about supermundane, infinite Existence can lead the consciousness out of its prison, but it is difficult to correlate the supermundane with the earthly in human understanding.

Who can remain free of distress from illusory contradictions? Who will accept the fact—"the higher, the more difficult?" Who will not bemoan that the approach to the Beautiful is not easy? True, illumination can be instantaneous, but this does not mean that the path ahead will be easy. In the ordinary earthly sense, man in approaching cognition already facilitates his path, but this should be clearly defined. Cognition reveals the paths, yet it would be faint-hearted to presuppose the easing of the path. Each joy creates a new care, thus the complexity of perceptions grows.

Speaking about the Subtle World, people rejoice that there thought will be the sole motive power. Correct, and not at all difficult to say, but is it easy to act by means of thought? For such actions one must know how to think. One must love the process of thinking. In the midst of every activity time must be found for the cultivation of thought. Besides, one must distinguish thought conceived by egoism from thought about the Common Good.

512. Conscious transmission of thought at a distance is still in an embryonic stage. Each undertaking in this direction is to be welcomed, but it will carry little weight for the broad masses. Therefore, together with experiments, lectures about thought-energy should be organized widely.

Brotherhood is primarily a School of Thought.

513. The consciousness of man is the meeting place of all the worlds. In waves of harmonies, in visions, in sensations, all worlds draw together. A treasure-trove has been entrusted to man—has it been well guarded? The cosmic knock may resound, and woe to those who shall not receive the guest.

People think that the knock of the far-off guest is something abstract; yet does not the physician know about a disorder in the organism which results from indefinable causes? Commonness of speech presupposes illness of the soul. There are many such illnesses!

514. There existed a method of cure by means of natural emanations. Instead of internal dosage, the sick were surrounded with appropriate minerals or plants. Of course, such a method presupposed a subtlety of receptivity. But if people wear magnetic rings and use local applications of the leaves of plants, the

surrounding substance will also be useful. One must not assume that the contact of metals and the proximity of certain plants do not act upon man. People consider such sensations idiosyncrasies, nevertheless the properties of minerals and plants are indisputable. People may become intoxicated from a single sniff of alcohol; they become feverish when approaching certain plants—one may notice everywhere the reaction to emanations. This field of man's interrelationships should be investigated.

515. Not only was levitation well known in remote antiquity but it was also understood rationally. Amid the ignorance of the Middle Ages even a thought about flying apparatuses was regarded as sorcery. Only now do people look back with pity at the ignorance of the Middle Ages and accept aviation as something natural. But did the grandfathers of the present generation think similarly?

I mention this because many attainments are as yet in a state similar to that of the Middle Ages. In a short time auras will be photographed, thoughts will be measured, there will be apparatuses to determine emanations, yet at present only a few people admit such possibilities. Not so long ago television was an idle tale, people considered it inaccessible, yet they promptly accepted it as a factor in their comfort. One may surmise that the measuring of thought and determining of emanations will not be pleasing to many who have become accustomed to concealing even their own age.

Thus, let us ponder on the happy possibilities that will increase with acceptance of the concept of Brotherhood.

516. The physicians of antiquity determined the quality of emanations by the application of plants and metals. They also made use of certain breeds of dogs

which were very sensitive to the emanations of man. But nowadays the simplest apparatuses, such as an electrical machine, will record on a screen the rhythm and quality of emanations.

517. It is unthinkable not to sense the tension of the cosmic currents which absorb the psychic energy. There may be apparent a certain drowsiness, there may be absent-mindedness, as it were, there may be involuntary irritation—it is instructive to observe these signs that accompany the absorption of energy. People are inclined to attribute them to their own indisposition, but let us not forget the external causes.

518. He who wishes to damage a stringed instrument bangs upon the strings with malice in order to break them and bring the instrument into complete disarray. Does not the same thing take place when a hostile force intrudes for the purpose of upsetting the rhythm of labor? Only true workers understand the significance of rhythm; they know how difficult it is to attain such rhythm. Its violation is sometimes equivalent to murder or poisoning. The enemy's hand actually stretches forth to destroy this, one of the most refined achievements of man.

The ignorant will say that strings are easily replaced. But even the usual strings are chosen with care by a musician. Far more subtle is the structure of the rhythm of labor. Such destruction cannot be remedied. The Brotherhood is particularly concerned with the preservation of labor in its best rhythm. Likewise, in all communities people should learn to mutually safeguard labor; therein will be expressed the lofty measure of reciprocal respect.

519. Do not think that many understand the beautiful consonance of labor. Moreover, not many understand the distinction between joint and individual

labor; for most it is merely a contradiction, whereas it is but evolution. People must not lose individuality, yet in a chorus each voice contributes to the common success; and with this realization one must keep in mind the fundamentals of Brotherhood.

520. Throughout the world, seek Brotherhood in everything. It is to no purpose to think that the higher concepts enlighten one only in exceptional cases.

521. It is significant that physical exertion sometimes creates a particular clarity of thought. The same thing occurs through reaction to cold or heat. Does this not signify that thought is energy? The affirmation of thought, as well as the measurement of energy will yield many new discoveries. Many particular manifestations are concomitant with the unification of thought. You have read about manifestations which were magnified owing to the quantity of people present. It can hardly be claimed that all those present were thinking in unison. This means that the energy of thought acted as such. The current of energy assisted the participation of the forces of the Subtle World. At each gathering of people one may notice a special condensation of helpers from the Subtle World. Let us hope that the thoughts of people will attract good helpers. In its unified thinking Brotherhood creates a powerful current of Good.

522. Someone found a spring of healing water. He was carrying some of it in a vessel, and in his joy he spilled the precious fluid. Not every effort helps thinking, otherwise all prize fighters would become thinkers. It is useful to apply co-measurement everywhere.

523. Thought about help is especially useful. He who is himself in need and in straitened circumstances thinks of helping others; such self-abnegation is a great touchstone.

524. In different epochs there have appeared particular themes and symbols, which could not have been regarded as the work of individual creators. They remained as signs of the entire epoch. At present the subject of Atlantis is being particularly mentioned. Quite independently, in different parts of the world people have recalled forgotten cataclysms. Let us not consider these remembrances as threats. We are far from menaces. We may remind and caution, but not one of Us makes use of the dark force of suggestion through terror. Free will remains the distinctive quality of man. It is to be regretted if this marvelous energy propels madmen into an abyss. One can take warning measures, but it is inadmissible to break the law of free will. In the course of the fate of Atlantis one may see that plentiful forewarnings were issued, but the madmen did not listen. Likewise, in other epochs reminders can be perceived.

525. The Atlanteans had mastered aviation, they knew how to crossbreed plants, they employed powerful energies, they knew secrets of metals, they excelled in deadly implements of war. Are not these achievements reminiscent of some other ages?

526. The rapprochement of the worlds will proceed under the sign of science. One should realize that many details of the great process appear to be disconnected and unexpected. Indeed, this seeming disconnectedness only appears as such to the human eye. In reality, the system of manifestations is quite exact. Let the most diverse scientists carry out their observations. It is obvious that at no time up to the present have quite so many phenomena been taken note of by scientists. Let them, for the time being, be accepted as utilitarian; the main thing is that these observations be recorded on the pages of science. Eventually these fragments will be brought together in one system. Thus, out of disparate facts broad domains can be established, subject to scientific determination.

527. The current of thought is sometimes subjected to the most unexpected influences and intrusions. A truly honest thinker will not conceal the fact that the discipline of thought may be disturbed at times by extraneous influences. Besides, the force of impact can be so powerful that the original thought completely changes direction. Let us not speculate why such a reaction takes place. May be the force of the thought attracts other similar complements? May be a crossing of cosmic currents takes place? The main thing is that an outside energy obviously exerted its influence. Such observations often take place in the Brotherhood.

528. All efforts must be made to engage the cooperation of science.

529. Habit is second nature—a wise proverb indicating to what an extent habit dominates man. Precisely, habits render a man immobile and unreceptive. One can suppress habits, but it is not easy to eradicate them. People are continually encountered who boast of their victory over habits. But observe the daily routine of such victors, and you will find them slaves of habit. They have become so imbued with habits that they do not even feel the weight of such a yoke. It is especially tragic when a man is convinced that he is free, whereas he is really shackled in the fetters of his habits. It is most difficult to cure a sick man who denies his illness. Each one can name such incurable ones among people known to him. Yet in order to assimilate the concept of Brotherhood, mastery of existing habits is indispensable. Under habits We have in mind not the service for good, but the petty habits of selfhood.

It is Our custom to test those who are approaching

the Brotherhood on liberation from habits. Such testings must be unexpected. It is best to begin with small habits. Man is often concerned with defending them more than anything else. They are considered to be natural qualities, like birthmarks. Yet the newly born have no habits. Atavism, the family, and school foster the growth of habits. In any case, a routine habit is an enemy of evolution.

530. Through realization of true values routine habits will be rendered insignificant. The best liberation comes through a comparison of insignificance with greatness. It must not be thought that one should not speak about the small on the way to Brotherhood. It is justly regrettable that the fundamentals of cooperation and community are not understood by humanity. The chief enemies of cooperation will be the small habits of selfishness.

But is it possible to think of Brotherhood if even cooperation is not realized?

531. Since the worlds are on trial, each particle of them is being tested. One may foresee that someone will be terrified at such a supposition. But only injudicious thought can stand in the way of welcoming the law of evolution. Through expansion of consciousness one grows to love this incessant motion; would it be better to remain in the unchanging prison of errors and delusions? On the contrary, it is much more joyous to sense the constant testing, which engenders the feeling of responsibility.

In each cooperation on the path to Brotherhood responsibility will be the basis of growth.

532. Evolution, being the beautiful law of motion, must be understood also in relation to the centers of the human organism. As a symphony requires changes of keys, so does the organism rely upon different cen-

ters. Such a change does not signify the dying off of one of the centers, but it is a sign of the development of the next possibility.

Pay attention to the formula—thought-heart. It will not be understood at once; let us not coerce anyone's thinking, nevertheless some will propel their attention in this direction—it leads to Brotherhood.

533. The ability not to coerce another's will is one of the most difficult tests. Compulsion does not produce a good harvest, and yet it is necessary to guide and protect on dangerous paths. A great deal of experienced and solicitous guidance must be exercised.

534. Non-realization of Infinity leads to many errors. Thus, people begin to imagine that Earth is the center of creation, or they attempt to measure and define the dimensions of the manifested Universe. In this they forget that the manifested is continually evolving. There cannot be even a single static moment. But people are so imbued with earthly measures that they attempt to subject to them even the immeasurable. Let us not obstruct any quests. We have rejoiced even at small stratospheric flights, however one should guard against improper conclusions such as those that represent Earth as the center of the Universe. Such conceit is not befitting an enlightened scientist. It may be that he considers each point of Infinity a conditional center, but more probably he simply does not realize Infinity.

535. Doubtless, many will disparage an indication about the continuous evolutionary process of all that exists. Yet even from the point of view of all scientists this process of perfectment is undeniable. Only the ignorant can attempt to hold everything back in a motionless state. They will act thus owing to their ignorance of the past and from inability to think about the future. Thousands of hypotheses may be advanced, but let them be in motion, about motion, and because of motion.

First of all, the Brotherhood tests those who are approaching on the realization of motion and of Infinity.

536. It is inadmissible to imitate the dark inquisitors who strove to confine the Universe in a prison of immobility.

537. Among the sayings of the classical world may be found some indications regarding the profound foundations of Be-ness. It has been rightly said that "sleep is like unto death." In these few words it is explained that both conditions pertain to the Subtle World. But this meaning has been forgotten and the idea of immobility of the body has been placed foremost in this conception; and yet, even in primary schools the proverbs of antiquity are being taught. At the same time one could point out the significance of words and thus implant many true concepts. To affirm truth in simple words is equal to the manifestation of an indelible tablet of the covenant.

Moreover, why be confined to the so-called classical world? The most pointed, inventive expressions may be had from remote antiquity, provided one knows many of the meanings in the ancient languages.

538. It is right to commend Ayurvedic medicine. It should be understood that many thousands of years left cumulations of experience and wisdom. But let us not, after the fashion of the ignorant, make a deadly separation between homeopathy and allopathy. Let us not forget the accumulated knowledge of China and Tibet. Each nation had to face particularly threatening dangers and took special measures to oppose them.

Thus, he who collects the best blossoms will be a victorious physician.

539. The Brotherhood was sometimes called a salutary Community. This definition has a dual significance. Actually, the Brotherhood is primarily concerned with curative principles and establishes them among its fellow members. Each brotherhood, as a true unit, will be in itself the carrier of health. Attention should be paid to how a way of life in common reciprocally strengthens the condition of the organism if harmony has been realized. This principle of mutual strengthening should be investigated by science. It is especially instructive to observe that even in the physical sense mutual assistance has a great significance. Since there can be insatiable vampires, there can also be inexhaustible benefactors.

A Brotherhood of Benefactors is an invincible Stronghold.

540. Can faith and trust replace the force of muscles and nerves? Indeed, life itself confirms this truth, but what faith and what trust! Man should not affirm that his faith has limits. Love has no limits, and likewise faith. No one will dare to say that faith can be manifested no further. Many will be indignant at the statement that their faith is insufficient, but at some time they will comprehend how much they could have increased their energy.

Brotherhood is a School of Trust.

541. Some will call Brotherhood an exalted cooperative. Let us not stand in the way of such a definition. It is essential that the concept of Brotherhood enter life, and cooperation is already near to the understanding of the broad masses. Each heightening of cooperation will thereby be an approach to Brotherhood. Let people ponder carefully upon those traits of their characters which contribute to the strengthening of cooperation. Precisely these qualities will be of need to them on the path to Brotherhood. Let us not renounce the feature of communal life if individuality will be preserved in it. Each cooperative must also safeguard the individuality; only on this condition can cooperation be multiform and fruitful.

Thus one can elevate oneself from Earth to the understanding of the beautiful concept of Brotherhood.

542. We call to calmness and at the same time constantly speak of battle. One should understand this struggle as an accumulation of strength through work. It is impossible to intensify energy without labor, and each labor is a battle with chaos. Thus, knowledge of the meaning of battle will bestow calmness.

There is no contradiction which is not subject to comprehension.

543. Let us comprehend likewise how essential is the elimination of injustice. It is necessary to be fortified in a firm resolve that injustice will not be admitted. If such a decision is firm, a new accumulation of strength will result. It is not easy to safeguard oneself against injustice; it can make its appearance in any of the details of everyday life. There should not be any small injustices; each of them already violates the basis of evolution.

Thus, on the path to Brotherhood let us safeguard justice.

544. The corroding worm of discontent must be ejected from each cooperative. Some will call it striving for perfectment, others will call it doubt. One may name many stratagems, but they all will merely conceal the unbearable feeling of discontent. People do not take into consideration whence comes this worm into being. It is terrifying to think how many undertakings are destroyed because of discontent. One should investigate whence it arises.

545. People are drawn toward the Brotherhood by their feelings, and bodily, but primarily in the spirit. And only in the spirit, in the heart, lies the true path.

546. In the transmission of thought at a distance, certain methods are employed that are not without foundation. In two rooms, both painted in the same color, preferably green, the same note is sounded and the place is filled with the same aroma. Such methods undoubtedly have significance, but only of an auxiliary nature. The power of thought depends upon calmness and heart-striving. This should always be kept in mind, because people too often place the will in the brain. Such a brain-sending can be interrupted in space by a still stronger current. In general, the subtlest receptivity is needed around the will and sendings of thought.

To isolate a clear thought, without incidental waverings, will be in itself a lofty discipline. In the Brotherhood attention is paid to such purification of thought. Speaking of Brotherhood, it is unavoidable to touch upon thought-sendings. The work of thought will function from small to great tasks, and the discipline of the heart will be required for success. Each heart is surrounded by anxiety, agitations, and tremor. One can overcome these tremors by addressing oneself to Hierarchy, not halfway, but fully; such an appeal is not at all frequent. Yet for the simplest experiments unshakable striving is required. Usually a swarm of tiny, malicious insects attempts to violate the purity of thought. All these petty ones must be subdued by brotherly unity.

547. You are becoming clearly convinced of the preconceived opinions formed by people who presume to be scholars. It is deplorable when a disciplined thought chooses a prejudicial path. It is dishonest to read a book with a premeditated condemnation. If such a reader has not yet experienced personally many indicative manifestations, the more cautious should he be in his judgments.

We primarily value reality, facts, and indisputable manifestations.

548. Blessed is true cooperation; in it is the element of space. As Infinity ceaselessly flashes out in each spark of an electrical discharge, so, too, common labor engenders limitless effects. Therefore, let us not call labor small and of no consequence; no spatial spark should be condemned by man. The quality of spaciousness should be reverenced as something supermundane. And so labor is a furnace of supermundane sparks.

Cooperation is beautiful, but even more beautiful is Brotherhood.

549. I affirm the concept of brotherhood; it reminds us of that Brotherhood which will always be the dream of humanity. So many lofty deeds are affirmed by a reminder about the Great Brotherhood. The thought alone about the existence of such a Brotherhood fills a man with courage. One must muster all one's courage in order to resist the onslaught of darkness. But what, then, will strengthen such superhuman courage? Precisely Brotherhood can bestow invincible strength.

550. Do you wish to glorify labor? Then show your capacity for it. Do not censure him who labors daily. Do not enfeeble yourself with disproportionate work; convulsion of the muscles is not strength. Thus, disclose to what an extent labor has become a vital necessity. Only then will your praise of labor be worthy of Brotherhood.

551. Do you wish to affirm unity? Then prove how

devoted you are to it. Show by your own example that you can proceed in united service. Thus, in antiquity, disciples were sent into far-off lands, in order to prove to what an extent they would not dissipate their accumulations during the various conditions of the journey. One may perceive how an unsteady consciousness falters at each casual glitter. Is it possible to affirm unity and devotion if each turn of the road can cut off the foundations of Be-ness?

One should not wonder that there is such a multitude of tests around Brotherhood.

552. Do you wish to be courageous? Then prove your courage in battling for Brotherhood. Assurances alone will not create courage, nor will praises affirm achievement. No preparations can be a guarantee of success. Courage is tested by unexpected obstacles. I have already spoken about courage; if I repeat it, it means that this quality is especially needed on the path to Brotherhood.

553. Do you wish to be a healer? First of all ask yourself if you have sufficient strength to issue it for help to your fellow-man. Indeed, ask yourself, Can I give without regret for myself? Prove that your strength can bring healing without the use of any remedies. We do not have in mind efforts of the will and suggestion, for the primary energy is self-sufficient. One should ask oneself about this on the path to Brotherhood.

554. Do you wish to give proof of your best quality? Ask yourself about it. Do not wait for an opportunity, because each instant provides many opportunities to display any quality; one has but to wish to disclose it. Such readiness will be the best garment on the path to Brotherhood.

555. Let us not be in doubt as to what to do in moments between labors. Let us not forget that each

particle of time can be used for higher communion. There is joy in that the thread of the heart can be in constant communion with the most Beloved. I affirm that the voice of love requires no length of time. As a field of grass is filled with different flowers, so, too, the calls of the heart are radiant amid labors; they signify approach to Brotherhood.

556. Communion, like fragrance, spreads far. If it is beautiful, the quality of broad dispersion is a blessed one. Let space be saturated with the best thoughts; many of them will join harmonious radiations. Though not all can absorb the full expression of thoughts, yet the beneficent substance formed by them will be a healing one. One should offer gratitude to the unknown Senders, who impregnate space with beneficial substance. Thoughts manifested in lofty communion are as a spring in the midst of a desert. Pursuing the direction of such springs one may find the Brotherhood.

557. He who adheres to the Brotherhood knows full well where the Ineffable begins. Do not attempt to break his silence when he has reached the limit of possibilities. One should not burden him with questions which cannot be answered without harm. Only ignorance can assume that it can assimilate each answer. Yet, there can be answers so incomprehensible, as if spoken in an unknown language, that the consonance of the alien words may appear to convey the wrong meaning. Great cautiousness is necessary during the contact with higher concepts, Brotherhood being among them.

558. Verily, one should not wonder when psychic energy involuntarily wends its way to remote distances, owing to urgent need. One should recognize such a state as unavoidable and help one's energy to strive in accordance with its magnetic attraction; let it labor usefully.

559. Throughout the entire history of the world, waves of attention to the inner forces of man could have been perceived. These waves are linked with the periods of evolution. In any case, a growing attention to the essential nature of man will always be indicative of an especially significant period. If, at present, there are observed particular strivings for cognition of the essence of man's forces, such aspiration corresponds to cosmic conditions.

560. Upon each piece of handiwork particles of the human substance are stratified. Not only the state of the maker's health is left upon objects but also his spiritual striving remains indissolubly upon them for ages. It is possible to render harmless the effects of poison or the traces of infection, but stratifications of emanations cannot be ejected. Therefore it is so important that things be created with good will. For many this statement will seem like a fairy tale, yet it is not rare for people to call objects good or evil exactly as people are called.

Life is in everything—thus teaches the Brotherhood.

561. It will be asked, Can so-called living corpses wander about on Earth for a long time? For long periods, depending upon their animal attraction to the physical world. Psychic energy will leave them, their radiations will become negligible, and a small apparatus will reveal the signs of death. These walking corpses easily fall under the influence of strangers. They repeat empty words of their bygone days, convincing no one. Physicians may vainly examine their aorta, pointing to a valvular disease of the heart. These corpses are sometimes sensed by certain animals. Often these corpses remain as heads of big enterprises, nevertheless their dead husks permeate everything therein. The walking dead are strongly attached to life, for they do not understand the change of condition. They fear death.

562. It will be asked how to distinguish one who has acquired great knowledge. The greater the knowledge, the more difficult it is to distinguish its bearer. He knows how to guard the Ineffable. He will not be tempted by earthly moods. The path to Brotherhood can be entrusted to him.

563. Those who can see will behold much. Those who can sense will hear much and will know how to meet unexpected messengers—absolutely the unexpected, though awaited ones.

564. The Brotherhood knows no rest. Let the meaning of rest be pleasing only on the physical paths.

565. The Silvery Tear—thus We call the lofty degree of readiness for tests. The first word recalls the silver thread, the second—the chalice of patience. One should constantly keep in mind that the concept of the supermundane lives side by side with the earthly concept. This consciousness is very hard to maintain, for even good consciousnesses think only along one line in the hour of testing. We should not console ourselves with the thought that the silver thread is sturdy; let us rather safeguard it as if it were something fragile. Moreover, let us not forget that the chalice of patience is easily filled to overflowing, even in everyday life. It is not difficult to pass judgment on another's circumstances. Tests of equilibrium should be carried out upon oneself. Each such victory will be in itself a true success. Life provides many an opportunity for such victories. Preserve in memory each such conflict, instructive processes of thinking take place in it. The symbol of the tear for the chalice of patience is not accidental. It is difficult to restrain one's indignation when one observes a senseless destruction. A complaint about the brutalities of people often runs along the silver thread. The Teacher will often send a ray of Light so that one can look into the distance. Only the telescope of the spirit can cover the judgment.

The sowing of Armageddon is sprouting, in it is to be found the cause of causes.

566. There are many causes of madness. Let us not exculpate ourselves merely by obsession, let us ponder on all the ugliness of excesses. Also, let us not forget that, owing to a desire to escape karma, breakdowns of consciousness may occur. Man, feeling the unavoidability of something, strains his will to such an extent that a darkening of consciousness takes place. Moreover, brain sicknesses can also occur. The reduction of insanity depends upon physicians. And too, the idea of cooperation will constitute a salutary aid.

True evolution will deliver humanity from madness.

567. People know of monasteries which have been in existence for thousands of years. People know of business houses which go on for centuries. Thus, people are agreed to recognize the fact-findings of the most diverse institutions. But only about the Brotherhood do they express various doubts. Any possibility of the existence of the Brotherhood is especially denied by people. There are many reasons why people so greatly fear the concept of the Most Beautiful. Does not someone fear that the existence of the Brotherhood may reveal his intentions? Or that he may be compelled to think about the good of his fellow-men? An entire arsenal of weapons of egoism is brought to bear against the peace-loving Brotherhood. Simplest of all is to deny the very possibility of the existence of the Brotherhood. Historical examples, supported by biographies, would seem to prove the existence of the Brotherhood in different ages.

But those who do not wish to hear are particularly deaf.

568. It has been said that each man carries his particular mission. Actually, each one who has taken on an earthly body is already a messenger. Is it not wondrous? It changes nothing that most people have no conception of their destination. This forgetfulness is due to a lack of realization of the three worlds. One may imagine the transformation of a man who recognizes the usefulness of his earthly path. Brotherhood furthers such realization.

569. Since each man carries his own mission, no one can be left without help—and so it is. But one may picture the distress and sorrow of the Guide when he sees how much his counsels are rejected! At each crossroad one may notice the conflict between the wisdom of the Guide and the light-mindedness of the wayfarer. Precisely in the smallest acts is free will manifested, and the Guide must bow in sorrow before this immutable law. But in the Brotherhood there can be no such destructive conflict, because everything is based upon mutual respect.

Freedom is the adornment of wisdom, but profligacy is the horns of ignorance.

570. Free will is a solemn bidding to the wayfarer. Before reaching the far-off paths, it is essential to give him the precious gift of free will. Each one may act according to his ability, he will not be constrained. But the wise one will realize what a responsibility he bears for the use of the treasure of free will. It is as if a purse full of gold were given him; it can be spent at his discretion, but an account would have to be rendered. And the Brotherhood teaches not to spend the entrusted treasure without usefulness.

571. Do not cause suffering—such is the Dictate imparted by the Brotherhood to the wayfarer. Let him realize how much easier it is not to cause suffering than to treat it afterwards. Should humanity renounce the causing of suffering, life would be immediately transformed. It is not difficult not to torment one's friend. It is not difficult to think of how to avoid inflicting pain. It is not difficult to imagine that it is much easier not to allow illness to take place than to cure it later.

Do not cause suffering—such is the Dictate of the Brotherhood.

572. Is it impossible to imagine how diversely is assistance given? It should not be thought that the means of assistance are limited only to the methods of charitable institutions. The best help arrives unexpectedly, but one must accept it. There are many meetings; there are many unknown letters; many unexpected books are sent, as if by chance. Over many years, he who possesses a searching mind will compare these strange incidents, and if he is not devoid of a sense of gratitude, he will send his thankfulness to the unknown Guardians. But a hardened heart not only forgets the help received, but even derides the unbidden Helpers. First of all, the Brotherhood inculcates the beautiful feeling of gratitude.

He who rejects cooperation inevitably falls into slavery. There are different aspects of bondage which should be recognized, otherwise the branded slave will think himself free and will even become so used to his shackles that he will regard them as a chain of honor. It must be understood that in human society there can be either free cooperation or slavery in all its aspects.

Brotherhood is a manifestation of highest cooperation.

573. Be not ashamed to reiterate persistently if you see that the salutary counsel is being scorned by the ignorant. It was rightly spoken about casting pearls before swine, but it was also spoken about building a whole mountain by the daily casting of handfuls of sand.

Understanding of counterpositions in itself leads to Brotherhood.

574. For some Our counsels are a reliable staff, for others an intolerable burden. Some will accept the Advice as something long awaited, whereas others will find grounds for discontent in each counsel. Man cannot understand how fully must the advice be in harmony with his consciousness. One cannot put into practice many useful courses of action merely because of their rejection. Good does not dwell with rejection. Good has an open door, it needs no locks.

Only in the Brotherhood can one learn about openness and secrecy.

575. Amidst millennia how can one discover the Founder of the Brotherhood? Nations call him Rama, Osiris, Orpheus, and many better names whose memory has been preserved by peoples. Let us not vie with them as to whom to give primacy. All these were tormented and torn to pieces. Contemporaries do not forgive concern over the Common Good. In the course of the ages let the Teaching be transmuted, and thus the scattered parts of the one body will be collected. But who will gather them? The memory of the people has affirmed Her who will apply her forces for the joining of the living parts. Remember the many who have toiled for the Brotherhood.

576. Eternal life is the most obscure concept from

the point of view of earthly thinking. Different people sometimes even belittle this concept into a prolongation of life here on Earth. What an error! Worlds will be renewed, yet the dwellers of Earth must remain congealed in the same garment! Is it possible for the Teacher to be concerned with the prolonging of earthly life? The Teacher thinks of the eternal life in all the worlds. But why, then, does the human heart pray for eternal life? The heart prays for eternal life of the consciousness. It knows that there is great good if the consciousness be uninterrupted and passes the ascent untiringly—thus teaches the Brotherhood.

577. One should not speak or even think about the Brotherhood if dissension, disturbance, and unbelief are felt. As delicate blossoms droop in a smoky atmosphere, so also the Images of the Brotherhood fly away amid irritation and falsehood. That which was still convincing yesterday can be distorted in the confusion of the heart. The clearest reflection of the Tower of Chun can be shattered by a crude touch.

Can the loftiest concepts be reviled by profanity? Such blasphemy settles indelibly upon the aura. It sticks fast to karma, as mud from under the wheels. It is not easy to wash it away. We do not threaten, but are drawing a comparison.

578. With what can one block the path of evil? Only with labor on Earth. Thought and work directed to the Common Good will be a strong weapon against evil. People frequently begin to verbally revile evil, but reviling is ugly in itself and it is impossible to fight by means of ugliness. Such weapons are worthless. Work and lofty thought will be the arms of victory—such is the path of Brotherhood.

579. Great beauty is contained in the acceptance of full responsibility. The vouching of the heart will

be that feeling of pathos which will uplift the primary energy. It will often be asked, How to increase this power? By the vouching of the heart. Conscious responsibility will be the beautiful impeller of energy. Thus does the Brotherhood teach.

580. "The stronger the light, the denser the darkness"—and this saying is also not understood, whereas one must accept it simply. It should not be thought that darkness increases from the light. Light reveals the darkness and then disperses it. The bearer of light also sees the dark shadows, which vanish at the approach of light. The timid assume that darkness will fall upon them; thus thinks timorousness, and the light trembles in its hands, and because of this tremor of fear the shadows come to life and play antics. In everything fear is a poor counselor.

The neophytes of the Brotherhood are tested upon fear. A most hopeless situation is shown to them, and one waits to see what solution will be chosen by the tested one. Very few will think, What is there to be afraid of since the Brotherhood stands behind us? Precisely such a premise liberates one from fear and brings to light a free, beneficial solution. But most often, before thinking about the Brotherhood, a man will promptly get distressed, irritated, and filled with imperil. A plea from one filled with poison will not be useful.

The Light of Truth is the light of courage, the light of devotion—with these words begin the Statutes of Brotherhood.

581. In the vast mountain region it is not easy to seek out the Abode of the Brotherhood. It is hard to picture the entire complexity of the massed mountains. You already know about the special protective measures. If there exist signs marking off the boundary lines, who will understand these marks? Even if there exists a description of the path, who will discover the indications in the complicated symbols? Yet even a thoughtless person will understand the reason for such cautiousness. In ordinary life people know how to protect a beloved man. Where there is heart and feeling the means will be found.

Let us safeguard the Brotherhood.

582. Some will say to you, "We are prepared to understand the Fundamentals of Brotherhood. We are ready to build up cooperation, but we are surrounded by such intolerable conditions that it is impossible to manifest greater readiness." In truth, there may be conditions that do not permit putting into practice that for which the heart is ready. Let us not expose innocent workers to danger; they can apply their abilities under other conditions. For a time let them construct Brotherhood in their thoughts. With such construction they can purify the surrounding space, and such thoughts will be salutary. But let them not fall into conceit, believing that it is sufficient to build mentally. No, the wayfarer will affirm the manifestation of achievement by human feet and human hands.

Likewise, although we will show solicitude for the overburdened ones, let us warn them not to give way to unwarranted fear. There can be no cogitation about Brotherhood when the mind is contracted with fear. The best approach to Brotherhood may be darkened by fear. Let us not forget that people are accustomed to being afraid of everything at all times.

583. Understanding of Brotherhood may come unexpectedly. People themselves turn possibilities into obstacles. Someone calls Earth a cemetery because death occurred upon each spot, but another considers this same Earth to be a place of birth because upon each spot life has been conceived. Both are right, but the first has imprisoned himself, whereas the second has been liberated for further advance.

Thus, look for co-workers there where they think about new life.

584. New life is in cooperation and joy for the Brotherhood. Do not think that thoughts about Brotherhood are already old. They appear eternally, as long awaited flowers.

At some time humanity will become weary, so weary that it will cry out for salvation, and this salvation will be in Brotherhood.

585. Each instant, someone somewhere is undergoing terrible misfortune. Let us not forget these perishing ones; let us send them thoughts of help. Perhaps people do not realize that afflictions are forever taking place, without end. In the Brotherhood they are known, and benevolent arrows are sent. Even if you cannot determine precisely the place of its destination, nevertheless send your salutary thought into space. It will find the right course and will be joined magnetically with Our Help. Beauty is found when, from diverse quarters of the world, thoughts of salvation come flying—in this each one will emulate the Brotherhood.

586. The primary basis of the Brotherhood was established, not as a haven of refuge, but as a focal point of thought. Since unification of thought produces multiplication of energy in a striking progression, it is but natural to bring together powerful thoughts. Such a base will be the point for diffusion of the thought of salvation. But people do not know how to be united in thought even for an instant. They break up their impulses by a multitude of petty thoughts. Some have tried blindfolding themselves and stopping up the ears

and nose in order not to be diverted by external sensations. But is the distraction an external one? It actually lies in an undisciplined consciousness.

Only Brotherhood can cultivate the will.

587. One may bow down outwardly before Brotherhood, while inwardly one may try to avoid Brotherhood with apprehension. There are many examples when hypocrites turned away from the concept of Brotherhood, yet bowed humbly down before it for the sake of display. Actually, fools are better than these hypocrites. Whom do they propose to deceive? Can it be the Brotherhood?

588. Let us look into the future radiantly; let us attract through love—such is the Dictate of Brotherhood.

589. Man cooperates oftener than he supposes. He is constantly lending psychic energy. During each materialization there is a discharge of ectoplasm, but aside from this substantial discharge, people give off energy at each contact and through this are joined together, as it were. Thus even a miser finds himself a giving co-worker. Still people forget about the constant exchange of energy. They do not understand this important action, for no one has told them about the radiations of energy. Only from the Source of Brotherhood have warnings about the great significance of primary energy begun to be widely disseminated.

590. It is essential to accustom oneself to subtle perceptions. Indeed, one should assiduously sharpen one's senses. Sometimes people try to accustom their ear to certain musical chords at varied distances. Even such a simple experiment yields unexpected observations. The very same chords will be perceived differently at various distances, which means that something exists, which intrudes and alters the quality of sound. If there can be changes even in such an ordinary perception, then how many reactions take place during subtle perceptions! People do not even think about them.

591. Harmony of labor is so necessary that special attention is paid to it in the Brotherhood. We advise having several tasks on hand in order the more easily to bring them into agreement with the inner state of consciousness. A better quality will be attained by such a method. It is too bad if a man begins to detest his work because of transitory currents.

I affirm that a wise change of occupation will heighten the quality of labor. Brotherhood teaches a solicitous attitude toward labor.

592. Because of the inexhaustible riches of nature it is difficult to isolate one portion from the whole. Verily, everything is so permeated with the all-embracing principle that even from a grossly material standpoint one thing cannot be separated from another. Take the tiniest insect, could it be studied apart from its surroundings, without all the causes of reactions and effects? The more difficult it is to study man apart from nature. All the branches of man's knowledge merely bear witness to their artificial subdivision. Biology, physiology, psychology, parapsychology, and a great number of similar subdivisions simply compel one to ask, Where is the man? It is impossible to study the great microcosm without realization of the primary energy. Only such a unified concept can advance observations into a grander scope of man's nature. In this one should also remember the lofty concepts which uplift the spirit; among the first will be the Brotherhood.

593. The peoples of Asia have preserved the memory of the Brotherhood; each in its own way, in its own tongue, with its own possibilities has preserved in the

depths of its heart a dream about an actual Refuge. The heart will not relinquish its dream about the Community of salvation, but will remember amidst sorrows that somewhere beyond the mountain peaks dwell the Protectors of the peoples. The very thought about them purifies the thinking and fills one with vigor. Thus, let us honor those who do not relinquish their best treasure.

594. In all ages the Brotherhood had special Ashrams. They could be shifted but the Center stands firm in the cragged Towers. It should be affirmed that the currents of the Brotherhood are constantly pervading the world. One need not judge as to whether they are successful or unsuccessful; such premature deductions will only reveal a limited way of thinking about the Brotherhood.

595. The thought about cognizing the manifestations from below or from above is correct. Usually cognition is acquired along with the growth of consciousness. Man raises himself with difficulty, as if climbing toward a mountain top. That which he observes hanging above his consciousness oppresses him. Many concepts appear to be difficult, and he begins to avoid them. But there may be another means of cognition—man heroically uplifts his consciousness and then observes manifestations from above. Thus, the most complex manifestation will appear to be below his consciousness and will be easily apprehended. The second means of perception is the path of Brotherhood. By austere and inspired measures it awakens the consciousness and leads it upward, in order the more easily to perceive the most complex manifestations. This means of uplifting the consciousness is especially needed in a time of pressure and cumulations. It can be applied in each sagacious school of thought, but it should be known as the path of Brotherhood.

596. A city of science will always be the dream of enlightened people. No one would presume to raise objections to an abode of scientists, where in peace and wise communion truths would be brought to light. Each learned worker would have the best equipment at his disposal. One can picture what discoveries would issue from general concordance and cooperation of all the branches of science! No one would consider the idea of such a city utopian. If only the means and good will could be found! But if one were to say that a certain Abode of Knowledge does exist, a multitude of doubts and denials would come tumbling out. And if to the word science one were to add the word Brotherhood, it will certainly be said that such a chemical combination is impossible. But who has said that science and Brotherhood are incompatible?

597. Precisely, Brotherhood is founded on knowledge. True science lives through brotherly communion—such is the Dictate of Brotherhood.

598. Allotment of office based on birth cannot exist in Brotherhood. A natural hierarchy flows out of priority of knowledge and preeminence of spirit. Thus, a most disturbing circumstance to humanity is resolved in the Brotherhood simply, without involving needless quarreling and friction. Where it is realized that priority is a great sacrifice, there can be no wrangling about earthly denominations. So much time and energy will be conserved by the principles of Brotherhood. Let us not becloud the luminous concept by the fact that it has been pronounced at times along with the misunderstood concepts of liberty and equality. Everyone understands the relative value of both these concepts, but Brotherhood based upon the heart's straight-knowledge will be unconditional. Thus, one may regard the Brotherhood as reality.

599. As bees collect honey so you, too, should collect knowledge. It will be asked, What is new in this advice? Its newness is in that one should collect knowledge from everywhere. Until now knowledge had fixed limits, and entire domains of it were kept under prohibition, suspicion, and in neglect. People have not had the courage to overcome prejudices. They have forgotten that a scholar, first of all, must be open to all that exists. There are no forbidden domains for a scholar. He does not belittle any manifestation of nature, for he understands that the cause and effect of each manifestation have a profound significance.

Brotherhood teaches unprejudiced cognition.

600. Let it not be thought by scientists that any censure of them issues from the Brotherhood. Scientists are Our friends. We do not call bookmen, full of superstition, scientists; but each enlightened scientific worker receives a greeting of welcome from the Brotherhood.

601. Likewise, let us welcome those schoolteachers who can find an hour to talk to their pupils about the dignity and responsibility of man, about the primary energy, and about the treasures belonging to all peoples. Such preceptors will indeed make more manifest the path of labor and achievement. They will find harmony between the preeminence of the spirit and the health of the body. They will introduce the book of knowledge into each dwelling. The life of such teachers is hard. Let there live in them the life-giving dream about the Brotherhood.

602. Preserve solemnity. Surround yourself with solemnity when you think and speak about the Brotherhood. Thought about Brotherhood is in itself a great communion. Thought that is pure and clear will reach its destination. But where words about the Brotherhood are dragged in the dust of the bazaar, do not expect a harvest. The whirl of curses will not be stilled; cognition of the forces of nature is not obtained amidst revilements. Long since did We discourse about co-measurement. Each concept requires its proper environment. Because of this, seek for the reason why sometimes a concept is exalted, while at other times it grows faded, becoming frippery.

Harmonious discourse about Brotherhood will give an unprecedented upliftment of the spirit if it be truly harmonious. Thus, let us apprehend all the qualities necessary for approach to Brotherhood. Once again let us confirm that a mood of solemnity will be the best guide to Brotherhood. The meaning of the word mood indicates that it is not external but internal, in a concordance of all the strings of the instrument. Such clear concordance is rarely realized.

At the crossroads people shout lustily about Brotherhood, but any discipline seems to be a compulsion. Only solemnity helps one to utter with dignity the beautiful word, Brotherhood.

603. Amidst deeply engrossing occupations you have more than once felt a sudden expenditure of energy. Even during the most absorbing labors you might have sensed an inexplicable absentation. A perceptive disciple values these flights of consciousness. He will have a fleeting thought, "May the Teacher help me to bring assistance where it is needed. May all go well with the world."

604. The assumption of personal superiority is one of the most shameful manifestations of the imperfection of the spirit. It not only corrupts all the surroundings but it also remains as the greatest impediment to improvement. It is essential to counteract such an ailment with a powerful restorative. Thought about cooperation and Brotherhood will be salutary in guarding against such a dangerous ailment, and will call forth new strength.

In the Brotherhood there can be no assumption of personal superiority, just as there can be no self-satisfaction.

605. An increase of criminality is observed everywhere. No one can deny that the most subtle crimes attract weak human minds. The usual measures of combating crime are not effective. Therefore, the hope remains that the principle of healthy cooperation may lead humanity into the boundaries of dignified labor, but let us also summon the principle of Brotherhood.

606. Determine in your consciousness whether the concept of Brotherhood serves the limitation or expansion of your possibilities. If someone feels even the least constricting influence, let him not come near the Brotherhood. But if the heart is ready to accept the advantages of Brotherhood, then the message will come.

607. Captives were formerly considered the indispensable attribute of the conqueror. Later it was realized that such barbaric customs are incompatible with the dignity of man. But let us see, has the number of captives really diminished? On the contrary, it has increased in all walks of life. Such abasement particularly strikes one's eye when one observes the prisoners of ignorance. It is hard to picture the throngs of those bound by superstition and various prejudices! The most demeaned slaves could not have been in a more bestial state than those bipeds shackled in ignorance. Only the most urgent measures of knowledge can prevent mass madness.

608. Suicides are on the increase. No one will deny that there never have been so many self-inflicted interruptions of life. It means that no one has told these unfortunate ones about the significance of life. No one has warned them about the consequences of their action. Are there among people none to raise their voices for truth and beauty of life?

Brotherhood has saved multitudes of people from rash acts of madness. Among the statutes of Brotherhood may be found an edict about curing soul and body. Many messengers are hastening to prevent madness. Sometimes they will be received by people, but not seldom a violent free will rushes ahead to pass judgment upon itself.

609. Imagination is insufficiently developed in people. They are unable to imagine causes and effects. They do not know how to picture to themselves the most beautiful possibilities. They have not been taught imagination and inspiration. The best strivings have been scoffed at, and people have been persuaded not to think. But those who know not how to think have no imagination. Loss of imagination is renunciation of joy.

610. Travelers may knock for admittance. Travelers could tell about the Great Souls who dwell in unfailing service beyond the far-off deserts, beyond the mountains, beyond the snows.

Travelers will not tell whether they have been in the Abode. Travelers will not utter the word Brotherhood, yet each listener will comprehend what Center of Knowledge is spoken about. The Sowers of Good go about the world when humanity is atremble.

People wish to hear about the Stronghold, the Citadel. If they will not learn about the statutes, they will nevertheless grow stronger at the mere message that the Stronghold of Knowledge does exist. The Lotus of the heart is aquiver at the approach of the dates.

Rejoice at the existence of Brotherhood!

When the consciousness is bedimmed, when the higher concepts seem far removed, at least ponder about unity in actions of good.

It is unthinkable to turn away from all that brings strength.

There can be no lasting labor in the name of dissension; unacceptable is dust at the threshold.

When you get ready for the long journey, wipe away all dust in order to leave a clean place behind you.

Thus, in all the manifestations of life let us remember about the Center of Knowledge and Justice—about Brotherhood.

AGNI YOGA SERIES

Leaves of Morya's Garden I (The Call)	1924
Leaves of Morya's Garden II (Illumination)	1925
New Era Community	1926

Signs of Agni Yoga

Agni Yoga	1929
Infinity I	1930
Infinity II	1930
Hierarchy	1931
Heart	1932
Fiery World I	1933
Fiery World II	1934
Fiery World III	1935
Aum	1936
Brotherhood	1937
Supermundane (in 3 volumes)	1938

Agni Yoga Society
www.agniyoga.org

www.ingramcontent.com/pod-product-compliance
Lightning Source LLC
Chambersburg PA
CBHW061639040426
42446CB00010B/1501